Catholic Realism:
a Framework for the Refutation of Atheism and the Evangelization of Atheists

by

Dr. Sebastian Mahfood, OP, and Dr. Ronda Chervin

En Route Books & Media

En Route Books & Media

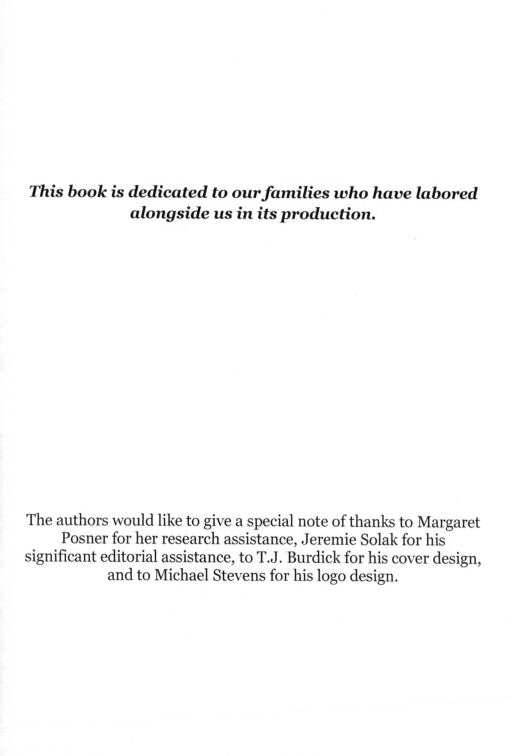

This book is dedicated to our families who have labored alongside us in its production.

The authors would like to give a special note of thanks to Margaret Posner for her research assistance, Jeremie Solak for his significant editorial assistance, to T.J. Burdick for his cover design, and to Michael Stevens for his logo design.

Catholic Realism:
a Framework for the Refutation of Atheism and the Evangelization of Atheists

Table of Contents

Foreword

"To be or not to be, that is the question." –*Hamlet*

If each century is an act in the drama of The Story of People on Earth, then we are still in the beginning scenes of Act 21. And it is time for some of us to start giving more attention to our lines. After all, we are each a player in this global theatre that moves through the pages of time.

Our lines—the words of our lives—cannot be said meaningfully if they are not understood in context: if we don't know the family history, the human history, of what has been said before us (or even about us), then we listen and speak (write and read) without understanding and without sense.

Some of us are quick studies, but most of us are not and we must rely on diligence to accomplish much of anything. Fortunately, we have friends to reward such diligence, and these brothers and sisters of ours are committed to helping us do our part in understanding reality and the drama of our lives: two such people are the authors of this book. One is a former atheist, and the other is someone whose dead faith sought daily to empty the cross of its power over him.

Ronda Chervin's childhood scene was atheism in a Marxist and culturally Jewish family on the East Coast. Dietrich Von Hildebrand and Company directed her to a window looking onto a different scene in which the people had joy and were not just acting. Her life has been directed by a call to help others discover that same joy which is an authentic dimension of the Christian life: her call has been a call to share.

Sebastian Mahfood's life was touched by the same Church and the same joy. While serving in the United States Peace Corps in Tunisia, this skeptic interested in keeping religious demands at a distance found himself in a scene not of his own design. A priest friend invited him to a church, and while there, Saint John Paul II shook his hand. The mystics and wanna-be mystics (like myself) will appreciate his retelling of the electric connection that opened his eyes to new scenes in his life: and he found his new lines to be old lines that never rust or lose their transcendent goodness, their reality. His call has been to connect others to eternal truths.

Solzhenitsyn famously said that "the battle line between good and evil is drawn across each of our hearts." Likewise, truth and falsehood are both occupying powers. The truth liberates us. Falsehood, confusion, and misunderstanding put parts or even or all of us in a kind of gulag or wasteland. Such a hell on earth was chosen by the Macbeths—who given every opportunity to live by truth gave up truth only to lose everything—from ambition to love.

Chervin and Mahfood seek the truth and show how it leads to love unending. They are good guides. Dialogue with them as you read.

So whether you are atheists or Christians, just curious or looking for arguments to tear into, this book will bring you clarity and understanding—on what atheism offers and does not, and about what Catholic Christianity offers and affirms.

In the end, we may still disagree, but we will not be able to easily say that we do not understand each other—that we do not know what the lines mean.

Jeremie Solak
Roscommon, MI

Introduction: The Daring Realism of Divine Love

"The event of the Incarnation, of God who became man, like us, shows us the daring realism of divine love. God's action, in fact, was not limited to words. On the contrary, we might say that he was not content with speaking, but entered into our history, taking upon himself the effort and burden of human life."
— Pope Benedict XVI, Audience, January 9, 2013
(*L'Osservatore Romano*, January 16, 2013)

Atheism is in revival. Many of the 21st Century characters lack a belief in a supernatural Creator. In response, we authors decided in the summer of 2012 to teach a course refuting both the old atheism, which had gained ground in the early 20th century, and the New Atheism, even more militantly anti-religious, which had risen to prominence by the end of that century. In light of the aggressiveness of the New Atheists, we endeavored in the summer of 2013 not only to refute the claim that God does not exist, but also to evangelize the atheists into the kind of belief (nothing less than an understanding that God exists) that could lead to faith (nothing less than an active response to divine revelation). We needed to articulate, in short, a vision of Catholic Realism, the idea expressed by Pope Benedict XVI in the quote above-- that the "daring realism of divine love" requires a response from us.

In pursuit of this end, we first collated our materials on the old atheists so that we could compare what they were trying to accomplish with the stated goals of the New Atheists. Once we identified our primary group of atheists, we surfaced texts from theists who provided strong refutations of their claims. It was at this point that we discovered that our commentary on both sets of texts had already formed itself into a publishable book that could be used to assist in the effort to evangelize atheists, and we were buoyed in our efforts by the love that Pope Francis expressed in his 2013 speech on the Feast of St. Rita, the Patron of Impossible Things,

> The Lord has redeemed all of us, all of us, with the Blood of Christ: all of us, not just Catholics. Everyone! 'Father, the atheists?' Even the atheists. Everyone! And this Blood makes us children of God of the first class! We are created children in the likeness of God and the Blood of Christ has redeemed us all! And we all have a duty to do good. And this commandment for everyone to do good, I think, is a beautiful path towards peace. If we, each doing our own part, if we do good to others, if we meet there, doing good, and we go slowly, gently, little by little, we will make that culture of encounter: we need that so much. We must meet one another doing good. 'But I don't believe, Father, I am an atheist!' But do good: we will meet one another there.[1]

What does it mean to "do good"? Pope Francis explained that the foundation for 'doing good' arises from natural law:

> The Lord created us in His image and likeness, and we are the image of the Lord, and He does good and all of us have

---

[1] Pope Francis, "Pope at Mass: Culture of encounter is the foundation of peace," Radio Vaticana (May 22, 2013), Online at http://en.radiovaticana.va/news/2013/05/22/pope_at_mass:_cultur e_of_encounter_is_the_foundation_of_peace/en1-694445

this commandment at heart: do good and do not do evil. All of us. 'But, Father, this is not Catholic! He cannot do good.' Yes, he can. He must. Not can: must! Because he has this commandment within him.[2]

Natural law, which is the participation of the rational creature in the eternal law, applies to all of us, regardless of creed; in fact, it is what assures that all humans are equal in dignity even if not in creed. An atheist is still a human person and is still bound by the natural law, which makes its presence known within his conscience. St. Paul explained this characteristic in Romans 7:15-16, "I do not understand what I do. For what I want to do I do not do, but what I hate I do. And if I do what I do not want to do, I agree that the law is good." He added in verses 19-20, "I do not do the good I want to do, but the evil I do not want to do—this I keep on doing. Now if I do what I do not want to do, it is no longer I who do it, but it is sin living in me that does it." In short, we are all designed to pursue the good and avoid the evil, but we have something within us that causes us not to do it, and that is sin, classically defined as turning away from the Creator toward the created thing.

Seeing the term "Catholic Realism" in various places in our 21st Century, we wondered whether that could be the name of a restorative synthesis for our new century. It would hand down the basic truths of 20th Century Catholic thought and could be an umbrella term for ideas of current thinkers and professors into a synthesis for the students we teach. When we use the term "Catholic Realism," then, what we have in mind is primarily what is "really" true in contrast to the many fatally erroneous ideas that abounded in the 20th century and persist to this day. Catholic Realism can also be considered in contrast to abstract ways of expressing truth that can be hard to teach.

---

[2] Pope Francis, "Pope at Mass."

Doctrinally, Catholic Realism advances a central tenet of our faith that Christ is both Lord and Savior. It is as Second Person of the Blessed Trinity that he is able to save us from original sin, personal sin and, ultimately, death. This truth is well-supported in the documents of Vatican II and in the Catholic Catechism. This truth is part of what is being disputed by atheism. Atheism is more far reaching though it denies the existence of any supernatural being, whether personal or not, to whom we owe our existence.

If the atheism of the 19th and 20th centuries intended to do away with the concept of God as a supernatural and creative being to whom we owed our existence, the New Atheism of the late-20th and early 21st centuries has waged war on the Person of God himself and by extension on all persons who adhere to their faith as, in the words of Richard Dawkins, guilty of child abuse for foisting faith in a personal God on the next generation. What we are seeing today among the New Atheists, then, is the *culmination* of an intellectual battle that has been going on for some time between theists and atheists. This intellectual battle is characterized on the one hand by those who endeavor to promote a sense of man's radical autonomy and on the other by those who endeavor to promote man's properly ordered relationship with God.

A Person: An Interdependent Unity

As much as this is an intellectual battle, then, it is also a spiritual battle. We Catholics understand the rational faculty of man to also be the spiritual faculty, which means that we know the relationship between the intellectual and spiritual life can never really be severed. This relationship can, however, not be expressed to its fullest. If one withers spiritually, one is also withering intellectually. Someone with a darkened spiritual life is going to find, necessarily, that his or her intellect has also been darkened by these obstacles casting shadows over it. He or she may even be annoyed by the fullness of the light being let in when the obstacles are removed, so accustomed he or she has been to working in dimmed and dimming light.

The only thing that enables us to pursue our intellectual work, though, is the grace of God, and when we turn our backs on our Creator for the purpose of fixing our attention only on His creation, we cast a shadow ourselves upon all we discern. We become the very obstacles that need to be cleared out of the way when we do not allow the light of God's grace to shine through us to the world. We can rightly say, then, that our study of atheism and New Atheism is a study of those shadow-casting obstacles that need to be cleared out of the way for us to fully live. We cannot reach our potential until we actualize what is real.

Gaudium et Spes, one of the sixteen documents of Vatican II that was promulgated as the *Pastoral Constitution on the Church in the Modern World*, explains that "[t]aken as a whole, atheism is not a spontaneous development but stems from a variety of causes, including a critical reaction against religious beliefs, and in some places against the Christian religion in particular." "Modern atheism," the document continues, "often takes on a systematic expression which, in addition to other causes, stretches the desires for human independence to such a point that it poses difficulties against any kind of dependence on God. Those who profess atheism of this sort maintain that it gives man freedom to be an end unto himself, the sole artisan and creator of his own history."

We saw this most transparently in the 1992 Supreme Court case called Planned Parenthood v. Casey, where Justices O'Connor, Kennedy, and Souter argued in part that "At the heart of liberty is the right to define one's own concept of existence, of meaning, of the universe, and of the mystery of human life" in its effort to safeguard the rights of a woman to her own reproductive health from what would otherwise, it argued, be dictated by the "compulsion of the state." Atheism, the Council argued almost thirty years before Casey, claims "that this freedom," what Saint John Paul II would call in *Veritatis splendor* 'radical autonomy,' "cannot be reconciled with the affirmation of a Lord Who is author and purpose of all things, or at least that this freedom makes such an affirmation altogether superfluous." Therefore, we may only affirm what is real.

      The Church, unlike the Supreme Court in the instance above, knows that it may only elucidate what truly exists. Affirmation of what is non-existent is non-sense. Affirmation of what is real is a mission of the Catholic Church. *Gaudium et Spes* further explains,

> In her loyal devotion to God and men, the Church has already repudiated and cannot cease repudiating, sorrowfully but as firmly as possible, those poisonous doctrines and actions which contradict reason and the common experience of humanity, and dethrone man from his native excellence. The Church holds that the recognition of God is in no way hostile to man's dignity, since this dignity is rooted and perfected in God. For man was made an intelligent and free member of society by God Who created him, but even more important, he is called as a son to commune with God and share in His happiness. The remedy which must be applied to atheism . . . is to be sought in a proper presentation of the Church's teaching as well as in the integral life of the Church and her members. . . . This faith needs to prove its fruitfulness by penetrating the believer's entire life, including its worldly dimensions, and by activating him toward justice and love, especially regarding the needy. . . . The Church . . . courteously invites atheists to examine the Gospel of Christ with an open mind.

Real dialogue requires such an examination. To be human requires such an examination.

Fifty years after *Gaudium et Spes* called for a sincere dialogue with atheists to address the diversity of reasons for seeking solace outside of joyful communion with their Creator, a Being Whom many not only don't recognize but also ridicule, we're confronted with a new kind of atheism, an atheism that seeks, according to Scott Hahn and Benjamin Wiker, political power for the purpose of eradicating, not dialoguing with, religious faith. Certainly, though, the New Atheists must take themselves seriously enough to know that there ought to be no need to eradicate what they do not believe is real.

These New Atheists are known to the younger generation – their names, Richard Dawkins, Daniel Dennett, Samuel Harris and Christopher Hitchens, are almost household names. Indeed, Hahn and Wiker call them the Four Horsemen of the New Atheism. These "four horsemen" consider themselves to be too rational to have faith in a transcendent God Who is responsible for all of creation, too rational to have faith in an immanent God Who has taken such a personal interest in his creation. Hahn and Wiker are spot on in their assessment of Richard Dawkins, which can be applied generally to all four of the new atheists– it's not that they are too rational; rather, it's that they are not rational enough.

Rational Freedom: Freedom with a Mind Toward Living

Saint Pope John Paul II, one of the principal authors of *Gaudium et Spes*, wrote three decades later in *Veritatis splendor* that we are freer when we follow God's law than we are when we endeavor to do otherwise. In explaining the concept of participated theonomy, he writes that "man's free obedience to God's law effectively implies that human reason and human will participate in God's wisdom and providence.

By forbidding man to 'eat of the tree of the knowledge of good and evil', God makes it clear that man does not originally possess such "knowledge" as something properly his own, but only participates in it by the light of natural reason and of Divine Revelation, which manifest to him the requirements and the promptings of eternal wisdom. Law must therefore be considered an expression of divine wisdom: by submitting to the law, freedom submits to the truth of creation. Consequently one must acknowledge in the freedom of the human person the image and the nearness of God, who is present in all." Human persons ought to seek to understand their range of motion—the range of their *raison d'être*.

In a culture that proclaims with the Supreme Court a radical autonomy essential to the liberty of man, the Church finds herself to be a counter-cultural phenomenon. She finds herself to be at variance, that is, with the culture in which she is situated. She finds herself defending man's true dignity in reminding all people of their proper place in God's creation, of their purpose for being called into existence, which is nothing less than eternal, joyful communion with God. Many people reject this message. They choose to live outside of joyful communion with God. When they do so, God does not remove from them his love even if their actions wound the relationship. This is evidenced by the simple fact that he keeps them in being, not only here on earth where persons who commit evil acts seem to prosper materially, but also in the afterlife where God has allows them through their own free will to choose their eternal destinies. When asked once what God says to the souls in hell, St. Augustine replied, "Only one thing – I love you." If God can say that to the damned whom he keeps in being, how much more so does he say it to the saved who are fully alive, according to St. Ireneus, only when they see God.

Living in a society that endeavors to shut itself off from God, we can understand St. Augustine's argument that the gates of hell are wide open, but no one wants to leave. Puffed up by pride, we insist on finding our own way even in the best of circumstances – so the New Atheists find in us willing sheep ready to be led into non-belief, and it is for this reason that we are pursuing our study of atheism – to help us understand its attractiveness and to learn how to guard against it.

***

Creation Accounts

We are looking forward to taking this journey with you and hope you find your faith is strengthened by this short book that we, through God's grace, have prepared.

We begin the introduction of ourselves, like the Book of Genesis, with two creation accounts. This first is written by Dr. Ronda Chervin, who grew up culturally Jewish but in a family of atheists. The second one is written from the point of view of a cradle Catholic who fell away from the Church during his teenage years only to rediscover his faith serving as a volunteer in a Muslim country for two years on behalf of the United States Peace Corps.

May the story of our own lives help you to understand our words and arguments in context.

***

From Atheism to Theism in the Catholic Church
by Ronda Chervin, Ph.D.

"Everyone believes in God deep in his or her heart, even atheists!" so think some believers. When this is proclaimed, I reply, "No! You only say that because you were brought up in a basically theistic home. In such families, even if no one practices the religion(s) of their ancestors, it is taken for granted that there is a God somewhere out there. And usually this God is conceived of as personal, that is, a conscious being capable of love."

There are, however, families of total atheists. Such people talk about whether God exists as often as you might talk about the possible reality, outside of children's books, of Dr. Seuss' quirky animals. And it was into such a family that my twin-sister and I were born in New York City in 1937 of the co-habitation of unmarried parents who met in the Communist party.

Of course, all communists were atheists. Most of them, however, in those times, came from homes where there were some remnants of religion, such as celebration of Christmas or Chanukah. Many such children of atheists showed up in churches or synagogues for specific rituals such as baptisms, bar-mitzvahs, marriages or funerals. At such times God was certainly mentioned. But in my case, I never participated in any ritual or set foot in any religious building until I was 20. And, I never heard the word God spoken in my home.

My mother's parents, Dr. and Mrs. Rosenson, were of German-Russian descent. They were professional German Jews who were invited by the Czar, at the end of the 19th century, to migrate in order to help modernize Russia. Once arrived in St. Petersburg, most such German Jews became fervent atheistic socialists. When news reached these Jews, who expected to live in Russia forever, that the police were rounding up suspicious leftist revolutionaries in the squares to shoot them, my grandparents, the children, and some of the Polish servants, fled to the United States. They arrived in this country in 1899 where they became part of the socialist intelligentsia of New York City. They not only detested their remote Jewish religious background, but also shunned everything to do with the Yiddish culture so prevalent in that city in the first half of the 20th century. Although my mother's German-Russian father, a doctor, practiced medicine among

Jewish immigrants in New York, her immediate family never spoke Yiddish, a mixture of German and Hebrew. Instead, they exulted in being free-thinking socialist Americans whose brotherhood was with all mankind, certainly not with ghetto Jews.

My father's father was of a Sephardic (Spanish) Jewish background. As a young man, he came to the United States from the island of Curacao off the coast of Colombia to study dentistry at the University of Pennsylvania. I can't remember ever wondering, as a child, how come a Hispanic youth would think of studying in Pennsylvania. Decades after the death of Solomon De Sola, my grandfather, I would meet a Hispanic woman in Philadelphia who had traced her own ancestry way back and discovered that these dental students were given scholarships to come to the States in order to help found and increase secret Jewish Masonic societies! My father, in his own old age, corroborated this. When I asked him about a ludicrous, seemingly paranoid theory some Catholics held, about secret Jewish masons, he replied humorously, "Well, Ronda, your grandfather, the dentist, was the head of the secret Jewish Masons in New York."

Jewish Masons left the faith of their forefathers and rarely practiced any religious rituals, substituting Masonic rites. Just before this grandfather died, he asked us, his only grandchildren, if in the public High School we went to they ever mentioned God. I think he was hoping there might be a personal God who could offer him the possibility of life after death. "Never is God mentioned at my school," was my truthful reply.

However, there was one person in our family who was totally theistic. This was my father's mother, a Pennsylvania Dutch (Deutsch, German, pronounced Dutch in English) devout Christian, who met my grandfather when he was doing his internship as a dentist. Grace Geist, an ethereal blond farm girl, was infatuated with this young Hispanic Don Juan, so different from anyone else in her small town near Allentown, Pennsylvania.

In spite of the influence of his Bible-reading, Jesus-loving, mother, my father one day in his early teens, stood up in the Presbyterian Church and announced loudly that he couldn't be confirmed because he had become an atheist. He walked out of the Church to begin his journey through Communist atheism to eventually working with the famous Madalyn Murray O'Hair on promulgating atheism throughout the United States. He enjoyed researching the lives of the Presidents to prove that most of them were atheists. He didn't know that non-Church-going presidents were mostly Deists (believing in a Creator God even if shunning main-line Christian Churches).

Whether my father's teen atheism came from the influence of his Masonic-Jewish ancestry grandfather I do not know. The effect of this stance, however, was to turn him totally against his very loving, affectionate, mother whom he regarded as a crazed idiot for her piety. My grandmother was rarely allowed to visit us lest she spread the poison of religion. But, for a reason I could not fathom, my sister and I were sent to visit our grandparents once a week. We had never opened a Bible, viewing the many books of Scripture on my grandmother's bookshelves as something disgusting; the way a Christian might view a collection of porn! From heaven, where I hope she is, she should be rejoicing that both these granddaughters became Christian leaders, albeit Roman Catholic. A charming anecdote told at her funeral back in Allentown, PA, was that she asked to be buried in a perpendicular coffin so that, at the time of the resurrection of the body, she could more quickly get out of her coffin and run to heaven.

In our house, God was never mentioned. My parents left the communist party over the Hitler/Stalin pact during World War II. My father eventually became an informer for the investigations spear-headed by Senator Joseph McCarthy. Just the same, my parent's rejection of Communism as a political theory and their staunch subsequent defense of democracy, did not include any interest in God or religion, still understood by them as something for those who were weak, stupid, or both. We little girl twins of ¾ Jewish but atheistic background went to school in the region of New York City called the upper nineties. As right wing political atheists of a Jewish ancestry, we didn't fit in with anyone around us: not with Catholics, not with the sprinkling of Protestants, certainly not with Orthodox religious Jews in full regalia, nor Reform Jews, nor Zionist atheist Jews, nor left-wing non-Zionist Jews. Later, as a Catholic, I realized that my desire to belong to an identifiable group, forever and ever, had a psychological as well as a theological reason. God, I find, uses everything, to win us to Himself.

However, when we were 8 years old, our parents separated for good. During this painful process we were sent for a few weeks to our grandmother's summer cottage in Fire Island. I felt miserable being dumped, the end not specified, in the house of this grandmother who loved us tenderly but whom I thought of us an idiot and a weakling. Seeing her opportunity to introduce us to Jesus, Grace De Sola insisted on pain of missing dessert, that we sing the famous lullaby "Jesus loves me, this I know, for the Bible tells me so, Jesus, loves me this I know, yes, Jesus loves me." Even though, in loyalty to our parents, we acted as if we sang that hymn only under duress, I never forgot the words. Was that the first time I heard you, Jesus, calling my name?

Fast forward: I was an eleven year old New York City girl at a public school. Once a week we had show-and-tell. Pre-selected students had to get up and display, say, a toy plastic turtle from a Christmas trip to Florida with a two sentence narrative. Amusing. No pressure except for the child who had to speak.

But one time something different happened. There was a pause. Probably the teacher was Catholic. There were a sprinkling at public schools, though they never talked about God, Jesus or the Church. One day at show and tell a quiet boy none of us paid attention to normally, came walking in wearing a long black robe with a white linen blouse like thing on top of it. He stood absolutely still, hands steepled in prayer, and started singing *Adeste Fidelis*. It was the first time I had ever heard sacred music. I listened in stunned, bewildered, but joyful, silence.

At the time I didn't realize that this lad must have been an altar boy at the Catholic Church. My knowledge of Catholics was limited, negative, though in hindsight, somewhat humorous. We lived in the same neighborhood that is depicted in West Side Story. Before the Puerto Ricans came it was partly Jewish and partly Irish Catholic. There were only about 2 Catholics at the public school because most Catholics children in those days went to the Catholic school. The only ones I saw on the street were incipient or actual members of gangs. Why did I think they were Catholics? Because in those days all Catholic girls wore crucifixes around their necks and the boys wore scapulars and sometimes also had rosaries dangling out of their pockets. Besides you could tell they were Catholics because they looked so mean. Since the girls also looked sexy, I used to think that was a mark of a Catholic!

One day I was walking home with my sister and a group of pre-teen boys circled us.

"So, what are you?

No answer from us trembling kiddos.

"Are you Catholics?"

"No."

"Are you Protestants."

"No."

"Are you Jewish?"

"No." (Our parents had never told us we had a Jewish ancestry.)

"So what are you?

"We're atheists," we answered proudly.

Having never heard of this category, they strolled off instead of beating us up as "Christ-killing Jews."

How did we find out we were Jewish? Well, the public school was 99% Jewish. So on Jewish holidays everyone had a holiday. When we mentioned at home that we were the only ones there besides 2 Catholics and 1 Protestant, our parents reluctantly admitted, "Well, you are Jews. You can stay home." Hurrah!

Affluent Jews sent their children off all summer to camps in New England. Being lower-middle class, after the separation of our parents when we were 8 years old, we went to the YMCA camp for 2 weeks. Although the YMCA was only nominally Christian, there was a tradition of having a Christmas celebration right in the middle of the July session of the camp! A nativity was assembled and the Christian counselors taught all of the campers how to sing Carols. If the parents of Jewish children got wind of this, they were allowed to have their kids excused from the practice and the "idolatrous ceremony of kissing the little "doll." But my sister and I were atheists, so our mother didn't mind if we learned Carols. Superstitious religious stuff was garbage as doctrine, but okay as just an old custom.

Hearing Silent Night and Come Holy Night sung, not on the radio, but live by beloved counselors, I was enchanted. Such beauty; somehow different from the beauty of secular classical music or popular songs.

Junior High School English class: the assignment was to write a page about what you want to be when you grow up. It had to be done on the spot. "How can I know what I want to be, if I don't know the meaning of life?" I wrote spontaneously. I don't think I would have remembered this precocious philosophical answer, a prophecy of my later choice to become a philosophy professor, had the teacher not graded it A plus and the word "profound" at the top of the paper.

After studying at Bronx High School of Science in High School, I went to City College and became a philosophy major searching for the meaning of life.

Then, in junior year, I transferred to the University of Rochester in upstate New York. Looking for pictures for my dorm room wall, I gravitated toward a cheap print of Salvador Dali's crucifixion, just because of its aesthetic value. Placed in a dorm wing of almost all New York City Jews, the other young women assumed I was a Catholic. Even though they were not very religious, they suggested I take it down since I was Jewish by culture if not by faith. I refused, without knowing why.

Like many, though not all, atheists, I was brought up to think the sexual morality of religious people was ridiculous. Out of fear of pregnancy, I had avoided going as far as sexual intercourse in High School. But being on my own in college, my great wish was to shed my virginity as soon as I could find some attractive young man willing to initiate me. By God's providence I didn't get pregnant, since I would surely have had an illegal abortion if I had.

One of my "friends" happened to love the music of Bach. One afternoon he sat me down in the lounge and made me listen to a Bach's *Wachet Auf.* I didn't like choral music at all, but I sat riveted to the chair listening with profound attention to the sacred song.

My third intimate male friend was a foreign student, in the philosophy graduate program. He was a German who had been in the Nazi Youth as a teen, but who had been saved by a Catholic priest from remaining in that terrible movement. Many of his friends became Catholic because of the ministry of the priest. He did not become a Catholic, but he somehow believed that Catholicism was the only salvation! He hoped to become a Catholic someday after sowing his wild oats. This man started feeding me apologetic books from G. K. Chesterton to Karl Adam. Not having ever read the New Testament, I hardly understood a word of these treatises. But something stuck, because I started wanting to meet Catholics even after my relationship to the German broke up.

During a trip, a friend wanted to visit the National Museum of Art in Washington, D.C. Hanging on a wall was Dali's Last Supper. I didn't like the picture at all from an aesthetic point of view, but I felt glued to the spot. I stared and stared at the table and the Christ, feeling mystically drawn into it. Fifteen minutes later my Jewish friend had to drag me away.

Majoring in philosophy had been my way of searching for truth. In the secular universities I attended, skepticism was so much in vogue that by a year of graduate school I felt hopeless. Where was truth? Where was love? Why even live? In this frame of mind, Thanksgiving vacation in NYC, 1958, my mother, who never watched TV during the day and never surfed channels, turned on a program called The Catholic Hour. The guests were Dietrich Von Hildebrand and Alice Jourdain, soon to become Dietrich Von Hildebrand's second wife. (He was a widower.) They were talking about truth and love. Spontaneously, I wrote a letter to them c/o of the station telling them of my unsuccessful search for truth.

It turned out they both lived on the West Side of NYC: Alice 2 blocks from me and Dietrich 10 blocks from me. Alice invited me for a visit. Her roommate, Madeleine (later to become the wife of Lyman Stebbins founder of Catholics United for the Faith) met me at the door and ushered me into a small room. There was this very European looking woman (she came from Belgium during World War II) who looked at me with such intense interest I was immediately drawn into her heart. She suggested I sit in on classes of Dietrich Von Hildebrand and Balduin Schwarz, his disciple, at Fordham University. In case you do not know about the life of Von

Hildebrand, he was a German philosopher who stood up against Hitler, fled to the United States during the War, and became one of the greatest philosophers of the 20th Century. (For more about his writings, google Dietrich Von Hildebrand)

I sat in on a few classes. What impressed me most was not the ideas of these Catholic philosophers which I didn't understand very well, but their personal vitality and joy. Drawn to this joy, as well as the loving friendliness with which everyone in this circle of Catholics moved out to greet a newcomer, I quickly switched from Johns Hopkins to Fordham to continue my graduate studies. The wife of Balduin Schwarz, one of my professors, was a Jewish woman, Leni, converted from an atheistic background of German Jewish doctors. Her background, so much like mine, and her loving personality certainly also made my entry into this new phase of my life easier.

After a few months at Fordham, I could not help but wonder how come the brilliant lay Catholics and the brilliant Jesuits in the philosophy department could believe those ideas such as the existence of God, the divinity of Christ, the reality of objective truth, moral absolutes, and the need for Church-going. Obviously, my parents had been wrong. It was not only stupid and weak people who thought this way. What is more they could prove, in a few sentences, that the mind could know truth and that there were universal ethical truths.

You can read about such proofs in Chapter 6 of this book where we write about how Catholic Realism refutes atheist ideas about morality.

Studying with Dietrich Von Hildebrand, Balduin Schwarz and great Jesuits, I was immersed in thrilling refutations of the ideas I was brought up with. I was sad to think that I would not be able to study with these wonderful people during the summer, since they went back to Europe every year during those months. By now I found it also hard to enjoy my sinful relationships with cynical if interesting men.

Unexpectedly, Professor Schwarz suggested I go on a Catholic art tour with them that summer.

To understand the miraculous character of the events that follow you have to know I hated all but modern art. This was owing to forced trips to museums as a child. I liked colorful impressionistic pictures but nothing earlier than the 20ᵗʰ century, and certainly not old-fashioned Catholic art. And, even though by now I thought there was truth, I had no knowledge of God, Christ, or the Church and no interest in learning more. So, my only reason for going on the tour was to cling to my dear new friends.

The first miracle came when I saw Chartres Cathedral in France. I looked at the amazing shape of that Church with the beautiful stained glass windows and I started to cry. The line from Keats: "Beauty is truth, truth is beauty," came to mind and I asked myself, "How could this be so beautiful if there is no truth to it, just medieval ignorance?"

The pilgrims on the Catholic Art Tour all went to daily Mass. Out of curiosity, I started going. Seeing my noble wise philosophy professor on his knees astounded and disgusted me. I wanted to jerk him up and say no man should kneel. "You are the captain of your soul, you are the master of your fate."

Finding out that I had never read the New Testament, my god-father to be, searched through bookstores in Southern France until he found a New Testament in English for me.

Second miracle: on the tour bus, reading the Gospels without understanding much, I fell asleep. I had a dream. There was a large room with tables. Jesus and Mary were sitting backs to the wall. Mary beckoned me and said in Hebrew "Come sit with us." (I don't know Hebrew but in the dream I did.)

Third miracle: I got the impulse to kneel on the floor of the hotel and say a skeptic's prayer I thought my professor had told me as a joke:

"God, if there is a God, save my soul, if I have a soul."

The next day we hit Lourdes. My godparents to be, the Schwarz's, were praying that I would not be put off by the rows of trinket vendors. I said, "I'm used to 42nd St., nothing bothers me." Fourth miracle: I was touched to the core by the Immaculate Mary hymn of the pilgrims sung in candlelight procession in many languages.

Fifth miracle: again, the art I thought I hated, was used by God to reach me. In a museum in Florence I saw Da Vinci's unfinished Nativity. I looked at the Virgin Mary, so simple, pure, and sweet, and I wept. She had something I would never have: purity! For the first time I thought of myself as a sinner. I felt impelled to tell my mentors, sure they would banish me. Of course, they didn't. Jesus came to save sinners.

Sixth miracle: The face of Christ in a tapestry of Raphael came alive, not for the others, but just for me! In this way, I experienced the divine nature of Christ before even becoming acquainted with arguments for God's existence. These arguments did impress me later on.

Seventh miracle: the tour included viewing Pope Pius XII at St. Peter's. I had dreaded being bored at museums, but having to be in a crowd watching the Pope, who I thought of vaguely as dressed up in the gold that belonged to the poor, was more than I could stand. I would go shopping instead. My mild professor insisted I go. So I went. At the end of the ceremony the Pope was blessing the disabled and sick. It was hard to see him because of the crowd. My rather old not very strong god-father to be lifted me up so I could see the charity of the face of the Holy Father. Pope Pius XII had exactly the same expression in his eyes, as the living face of Jesus from the tapestry.

Stunned by this profusion of supernatural happenings, but too much a thinker to proceed on that basis only, I studied books like C. S. Lewis' *Mere Christianity*. Lewis' famous chapter was an intellectual turning point. He shows that it is no good fence-sitting by deciding Jesus was just a wonderful man or a prophet. When a man claims to be divine he is either really God, insane or a liar? Since no one thinks Jesus was insane or a liar, he must have been divine. Reading books of Chesterton and Cardinal Newman made becoming a Catholic seem inevitable.

January 4, 1959, at 21, I was baptized. There has never been a moment in my life when I have regretted being a Catholic. Later my twin-sister, mother, and husband became Catholics, making us into a sort of Hebrew-Catholic family. In the last decade of his life, my father used to say that having worked so long with atheists he did not want to call himself an atheist anymore because they were just as bad as Christians! However, just before he died I handed him a copy of a biography of Abraham Lincoln with post-its on all the pages mentioning how much he believed in God even though he didn't go to Church. I met some neighbor friend of his, years after his death, who told me that he had talked to a priest just before his final heart attack!

The way God saved them and me during the rest of my long life can be found in my autobiography, *En Route to Eternity,* and also in other books by me that you can find at www.rondachervin.com and www.enroutebooksandmedia.com.

***

Away and Back Again in the Catholic Church
by Sebastian Mahfood, OP, Ph.D.

This creation account is written from the point of view of a cradle Catholic who fell away from the Church during his teenage years only to rediscover his faith serving as a volunteer in a Muslim country for two years on behalf of the United States Peace Corps.

For my own story, my father departed from the Catholic Church a month after his divorce in order to remarry since he had no basis for an annulment. Though we children were placed in a Catholic school soon thereafter, he had stopped taking an active role in our religious upbringing. A year and a half later, we left the Church altogether when he moved us from our home in East Texas to pursue work in southern Florida. We left the Catholic middle school in the middle of my 8th grade year, which meant that my confirmation would be deferred for what turned out to be almost a decade later.

A few years later, after we had returned to East Texas, my father and step-mother joined a local Baptist church in the hopes that this move would revive the sense of faith within the family, but I remained, at the age of 18, unconvinced of the need for further conversion. I had by that point no real reason to leave the Catholic Church even though I had not been attending mass for almost half a decade. My Catholicism was something that I took for granted, content only in my possessing a Catholic baptism as the foremost excuse for my not submitting to a re-baptism at the hands of the Baptists. If I had no reason to leave one church, I equally had no reason to join another. This attitude persisted until I entered the Peace Corps and encountered a people deeply moved by their own faith. I found myself having to daily answer the question of why I did not want to become a Muslim. The conversations went something like this:

"Inti muslim willa messehee?" ("Are you Muslim or Christian?")

"Christian," I would reply.

"Why don't you become a Muslim?"

"Because I know that Jesus loves me."

"Oh, we have Jesus, too. He is one of our greatest prophets."

"I believe he is more than a prophet."

"Oh? How so?"

At this point, I would usually get stuck. I could say that I believed that Jesus was the second Person of the Divine Trinity, but I really had no vocabulary to explain what I meant by that or that Christians did not worship three Gods. Some of my interlocutors would even count on their fingers, "Now, you say, God the Father, God the Son, and God the Holy Spirit, right?" "Right," I would affirm. "That's three Gods you've just counted. God is one!"

Through conversations like these, I realized I really could not fall back on the kinds of excuses I had given to the Baptist minister at every weekly baptism call when the "I believe I'm already baptized" line consistently produced such great results for me. The Muslims meant business. They wanted to know the content of my faith, and when I examined it, I found that there was little there but the memory of my elementary school catechism.

I admired, of course, their sincerity in trying to turn me into a better man of faith. I was intent on demonstrating that I already had a strong Christian faith, and for no better reason than to not become a Muslim. I knew I had to be able to explain to any Muslim who would press me on the issue why, on that day, I was still certain that I wanted to remain a Christian. I did not pursue my faith, then, for the purpose of proclaiming the Gospel or even of engaging in apologetics. I pursued it in order to find a magic escape formula that would work sure and certain each time someone would try to get me to say, "There is no God but Allah, and Mohamed is his prophet."

As the thought was forming in my mind that I would need to find a book – but where in the Muslim libraries would I find such a thing? - God responded by sending me a person. Fr. Jerome Thompson, a diocesan priest from Milwaukee on loan to the White Fathers in Tunisia, sat down next to me at a dinner party at the American ambassador's home and with the alacrity of any Muslim initiated the faith question – where was I confirmed?

"Confirmed?" I asked. "I haven't been."

"No problem," Fr. Jerry simply said. "We can handle that here before you end your volunteer service." Apparently, he was used to being a fisher of men.

I saw in this at the time little more than an opportunity to get some sound bite responses to my Muslim evangelists and so began on a two-year program of study concerning the content of my faith. I met with Fr. Jerry on almost every trip I made to the capital city from the university town of Kairouan where I had been stationed. He gave me books and discussed their content with me. He taught me about the history of the Church in North Africa, about St. Augustine, about the White Fathers and the French colonialists to whom the Church had once ministered in great numbers before the Tunisians received their independence in 1956. The important part in all this is that he engaged me in dialogue on a regular basis. He taught me not only my faith but how to share it with others.

In April of 1996, when I was 24 years old and just wrapping up my two-year tour of duty, two significant landmarks occurred in my life. The first was the visit of Saint John Paul II to the capital city of Tunis with a follow-up to Carthage to pray at the amphitheater where Sts. Perpetua and Felicity were killed. Fr. Jerry had found me two tickets to the Pope's mass celebration at the Cathedral, and I invited a fellow Peace Corps Volunteer named Stephanie Olson to accompany me. (Two and a half years later, Stephanie and I married, and we now have two children, Alexander, born in 2004, and Eva Ruth, born in 2008.) My tickets gained us access to the front of the Cathedral, in the standing area just behind the seated dignitaries, and when the Pope entered the Church he began crisscrossing his way up the aisle, taking hands and dispensing blessings on his way to the presider's chair. He took my hand, reader, and I felt a surge of energy at his blessing. I had a sense at that moment that God was stepping into my life in a new and profound way. The Holy Spirit had touched me that day.

The second big event that April was my confirmation. Bishop Fouad Twal, who would later become the Patriarch of Jerusalem – I met him again quite by accident – thanks to the prompting of a seminarian who is now Fr. Fadi Auro - in St. Louis in the year 2012 when he celebrated mass at Kenrick-Glennon Seminary where I was in my final year as associate professor of intercultural studies – presided over my confirmation in the Cathedral of Tunis. I entered the cathedral that day with a strong sense of accomplishment, and I did not at the time know that I would later become so intimately involved with the formation work of the Church. I considered my confirmation a kind of coming of age, a completion of something that I should have done a decade earlier. I did not know that it was the next step in my preparation for marriage, or that the woman who again decided to accompany me would in a very short time become my wife. The Holy Spirit had touched me that day, too.

Following these two events, my few remaining months in North Africa seemed anti-climactic. I came home to the United States and took a teaching job for a year at Texas Christian University. I then moved to St. Louis and worked as an adjunct in a few community colleges while I prepared for marriage. In 2000, a friend of my mother-in-law saw me building websites to assist in my teaching of developmental writing students and asked if I could talk to the liturgist at Kenrick-Glennon Seminary since he was in charge of an educational technology grant that had recently been received to update the institutional technological infrastructure and initiate faculty training on the new tools they would have available to them. I volunteered there for a year and was hired in 2001.

When the grant funds had been spent and I had effectively worked myself out of a job, the academic dean asked me to stay, offering me the faculty rank of assistant professor, which I would hold until I deposited my dissertation, entitled *Radical Eschatologies: Embracing the Eschaton in the Works of Ngugi wa Thiong'o, Nuruddin Farah and Ayi Kwei Armah*, in the spring of 2006. That summer, I was advanced to the rank of associate professor and held that position for the next six years. During that time, I founded the Catholic Distance Learning Network within the Seminary Department of the National Catholic Educational Association. The network was designed to provide certification in online teaching and learning to faculty in seminaries around the country for the purpose of our collaborating with one another's institutions on the offering of online courses. In the three years of the grant period, we certified about five dozen faculty members and organized two dozen course offerings affecting over a hundred seminarians.

I also continued my studies, completing a Master of Arts in Moral Philosophy in 2009 and a Master of Educational Technology degree in 2012. In the summer of 2013, I completed my Master of Arts in Moral Theology. These degrees serve the purpose of making me a better thinker with the Church both philosophically and theologically and more adept at designing online teaching and learning environments to assist in the cultivation of Catholic leaders for the purpose of evangelization. That came in handy in my work as Director of Distance Learning at Holy Apostles College & Seminary, a position I accepted as interim employment but which I took on full time after leaving Kenrick-Glennon Seminary in the spring of 2012 and held till the start of the spring 2014 academic term. In the spring of 2013, furthermore, I began a Master of Business Administration program, which I am on schedule to complete in the fall of 2016 for the purpose of making me a better steward of the institution I currently help lead as Vice-President of Administration, a position to which I was named at the start of the 2013-2014 academic year

My conversion story, then, began with my trying to avoid becoming a Muslim – that is, with my trying to avoid being drawn from a faith that was alien to me into a faith that was alien to me – and it continues almost two decades later with my having become the kind of person who proclaims his faith in public settings. My conversion from the city of man to the city of God, I strongly believe, was ordained by Providence. God, I learned, not only has a plan for my life, but he also has a plan for each and every person's life. All we have to do to begin our life's journey within that plan is open our hearts to his will and do whatever he tells us.

***

What We Intend to Accomplish in This Book

Dialogue for Enrichment Commanded

The present book will pursue its theme through teachings of the Pontifical Council of Inter-Religious Dialogue in its 1991 document entitled "Dialogue and Proclamation," for the simple reason that our being called into dialogue with one another was elevated to a commandment by Christ himself as St. John points out, "And he has given us this command: Anyone who loves God must also love their brother and sister" (1 John 4:21). Indeed, when tested with the question from one learned in the law as to the greatest commandment found in it, "Jesus replied: 'Love the Lord your God with all your heart and with all your soul and with all your mind.'" (Matt. 22:37). He followed it up with, "And the second is like it: 'Love your neighbor as yourself'" (Matt. 22:39). While Jesus is speaking from the order of creation, St. John explains it from the order of knowledge when he writes, "Whoever claims to love God yet hates a brother or sister is a liar. For whoever does not love their brother and sister, whom they have seen, cannot love

God, whom they have not seen" (1 John 4:20). What, then, is love?

Jesus provided a rubric when he said, "Therefore go and make disciples of all nations, baptizing them in the name of the Father and of the Son and of the Holy Spirit, and teaching them to obey everything I have commanded you. And surely I am with you always, to the very end of the age" (Matt. 28:19-20). It is to proclamation, then, that we are called as Christians, and the first step to that proclamation is to enter into dialogue with the Other, a dialogue that is fundamentally interfaith when we come against a professed atheist. The meaning of this kind of dialogue, according to *Proclamation and Dialogue* (1991), rests on "all positive and constructive interreligious relations with individuals and communities of other faiths which are directed at mutual understanding and enrichment, in obedience to truth and respect for freedom." So this is the quiddity of the importance of interreligious dialogue, which is a means by which we work with others to ensure not only peaceful resolution of conflict but also sustainable collaboration and harmony.

Diversity and Unity in Conversion

The second chapter concerns the types of atheists that exist along with some conversion stories of the old atheists. We hope that the new leadership of the faith will be able to kindle a love of God in the hearts of the New Atheists who have arisen among us with a political agenda of eradicating all faith. Among the different types of atheism are those which are scientifically based, all of which have in common a material reductivism to their science, seeking to place God within the container of that which is solely empirically measurable. Other types include literary atheism, in which fictional characters express their non-belief, Communist atheism, which sees faith as an obstacle to socioeconomic progress, various philosophical types of atheism that perceive faith as an assault on the powers of the mind, psychologically based atheism, which explains belief in God as due to a father-complex, and New Age substitution of the concept of some sort of energy for a personal God of Love. The New Atheism on the scene is in many ways simply following an older tradition.

The Key of Catholic Realism

The third chapter presents the main thrust of our argument, that Catholic Realism is the key to resolving the issue of atheism in all its forms. We explain that Catholic Realism is nothing else than an understanding of a personal God as necessary self-subsistent Being Who created out of nothing and through Love the contingent material universe. This is the God of Adam and Eve, of Abraham and Sarah, of Mary and Joseph, of the Patristic fathers and of the Doctors of the Church. This is the God of St. Thomas, Whose eternal law is comprehensible to humankind in the form of natural law, which is the participation of the rational creature in that eternal law, and revealed to humankind in the form of Divine law. This is the God of Vatican II, which sought a hermeneutic of continuity in the Church's two-thousand year tradition as it taught us how to understand the role of the Church in the modern world. God, in short, is He Who is, to use St. Catherine's explanation, or, to use God's own terms, "I am."

Nature and Revelation: A Shared Testimony

The fourth chapter discusses the relationship between science and theism, and it is our assertion, alongside that which has been attributed to St. Augustine, that the book of nature and the book of revelation were written by the same Author and cannot be shown to be in conflict when properly understood. The conflict between faith and science is due to the struggle on both sides concerning the proper response to material reductivism. We will demonstrate in this chapter the strong support given by the Church to the advancement of science and the strong affirmation of God provided through our scientific research through our exploration of the Order of Creation and the Order of Knowledge. In the first case, we understand that God created the universe out of nothing, which has been taught to us by the Magisterium through Scripture and Tradition, and in the second case, we know from the demonstrations provided by Aristotle and St. Thomas that we come to an understanding of the Creator through his creation as we apply our senses to the sensible world.

The Storm Cloud of Evil

The fifth chapter discusses the issue of theodicy, of the existence of a good God who yet permits the existence of evil in the world. This is a question asked not only by those who have no belief, like the atheists we read about in the second chapter, but also and especially by those with great belief, such as Job and Habbakuk. That God permits evil to exist provides us with no cause to condemn him, for he is the source from whom all things come, the one who brings good out of evil. This is an issue that was well-addressed in the *Divine Comedy* by Dante Alighieri concerning the tension between man's free will, our greatest gift, and the love that moves the sun and the other stars. C. S. Lewis also explored this issue in *The Problem of Pain*, as have other apologists over time. Our pain is real and profound, but the greatest pain is not ontic, or physical, but spiritual and moral; and it is brought about by sin, which is classically defined as a turning away from the Creator toward the created thing.

Life Giving Morality

The sixth chapter deals with morality and atheism, demonstrating how the atheist necessarily perceives morality in relativistic terms, embracing that radical autonomy about which Saint John Paul II writes in *Veritatis splendor*. Without an objective standard on which to base morality, any ethical system is as good as another; indeed, debates among the materially reductive ethical systems are those that glorify the partial experience of man whose worldview is built upon relativism and skepticism. Only a moral system built upon natural and divine law can aspire toward a realistic understanding of man's responsibility to man, for only Christ, who reveals mankind to himself, has provided a structure for the culture of life. All other structures participate in the culture of death, of man as the sum of his own solitary experience who chooses of his own free will to separate himself from the source of his being and exist as a thing apart from it. For those who choose otherwise, we find joyful communion with one another through the joyful communion we experience in God. People who choose not to connect with God will find it impossible to authentically connect with one another.

The Impact of Atheism on Heaven and Earth

The seventh and final chapter brings closure to the argument by discussing the impact of atheism on our world. Today, it is quite fashionable to be an atheist, so much so that theists may legitimately be uncertain of the presence of other theists in any given public gathering. This is why it is important for us to speak the truth to all persons in every way that will enable them to hear us. In so doing, we become a beacon of truth around which others might rally, and in our spiritual leadership over any group of which we are a part, we will find supporters there with us ready to take their stand.

We will also find atheists who have read the works of the New Atheists, Richard Dawkins, Daniel Dennett, Christopher Hitchens and Samuel Harris, and identify with them in one way or another. Though a new force in atheism, the New Atheists do not have the market for atheism entirely cornered, and many examples of contemporary classical atheists abound who problematize their goal of political activism to eradicate all faith as largely impractical.

What our possible futures might be under an atheist hegemony is the subject of narrative reasoning – whether the dystopian vision of George Orwell's *1984* where the power of the state crushes the soul of man or the utopian vision of Ayn Rand's *Anthem* where the soul of man overcomes the power of the state. We have only one future, though, under theism, and that is of infinite growth within an infinite being, the greatest blessing of our finitude, which can never plumb the depths of our Creator but only grow eternally in joyful communion with him.

Chapter 1: Affirming the Center and "Dialogue and Proclamation"

The 20th century was marked by severe polarities, not only in the world, but also in the Church. These polarities may rend our understanding and wills from what is true and good. The centering point for all of us in the Church, of course, is our Nicene Creed, which we recite at Mass, and here we call it to mind as palliative chorus:

> I believe in one God,
> the Father almighty,
> maker of heaven and earth,
> of all things visible and invisible.
> I believe in one Lord Jesus Christ,
> the Only Begotten Son of God,
> born of the Father before all ages.
> God from God, Light from Light,
> true God from true God,
> begotten, not made, consubstantial with the Father;
> through him all things were made.
> For us men and for our salvation
> he came down from heaven,
> and by the Holy Spirit was incarnate of the Virgin Mary,
> and became man.
> For our sake he was crucified under Pontius Pilate,
> he suffered death and was buried,
> and rose again on the third day
> in accordance with the Scriptures.
> He ascended into heaven
> and is seated at the right hand of the Father.

He will come again in glory
to judge the living and the dead
and his kingdom will have no end.
I believe in the Holy Spirit, the Lord, the giver of life,
who proceeds from the Father and the Son,
who with the Father and the Son is adored and glorified,
who has spoken through the prophets.
I believe in one, holy, catholic and apostolic Church.
I confess one Baptism for the forgiveness of sins
and I look forward to the resurrection of the dead
and the life of the world to come. Amen.

The Nicene Creed reminds us that both our present and future are rooted in one hope in Christ.

As human beings, we easily forget the importance and meaning of the most fundamental things. Reminding ourselves of fundamental truths is a way to renew our minds. Nothing could be more basic to Catholic Realism than this first proclamation of our Creed, which is divided into seven elements of profession, of belief, in eternal persons, realities, and communities:

1) God the Father,
2) God the Son,
3) God the Holy Spirit,
4) The Church,
5) The Role of Baptism,
6) The Resurrection of the Dead, and
7) The life of the world to come.

From this foundation, all theological doctrine flows: the doctrine of the Trinity, of the dual nature of Christ, of the active and passive processions of the Holy Spirit, of the nature of the Church, of the role of our baptism into it and of our future hope in the soteriological and eschatological realities expressed by the Magisterium from its understanding of Scripture and Tradition. We are bound to orthodoxy for freedom because only a real understanding of what is allows us to live meaningfully—to live in accord with what ought to be from knowledge of what is.

The starting point to a good Christian life based on Catholic doctrine begins with the Creed, and it finds its support in two cardinal commandments given to us by Christ in his response to one learned in the law. The greatest commandment is to "Love the Lord your God with all your heart and with all your soul and with all your mind" (Matt. 22:37); and the second greatest "is like it," namely, "Love your neighbor as yourself" (Matt. 22:39). To drive home the point that these commandments are the fonts from which the others spring, Jesus adds, not gratuitously, "All the Law and the Prophets hang on these two commandments" (Matt. 22:40). Our own minds should do likewise.

What more can we add but to summarize that God the Father sent his only begotten Son, Jesus, to save all of mankind and that the mission was a success. All we have to do is actively respond through the tools that God himself gives us--namely the theological virtues of faith, hope and charity--at the moment of our baptism. This simple but profoundly deep formula enables us to follow the Magisterium (which exercises stewardship over the Deposit of the Faith found in Scripture and Tradition) in pursuit of our faith. These things, then, are what we need to live and proclaim, and we should be wary of reaching beyond them out of desire to be thought erudite by our fellow man. Beatrice, in the 29th canto of Dante's *Paradiso*, warns us against this as follows:

> Christ did not to his first disciples say,
> 'Go forth, and to the world preach idle tales,'
> But unto them a true foundation gave;
>
> ...

Now men go forth with jests and drolleries
To preach, and if but well the people laugh,
The hood puffs out, and nothing more is asked.
(lines 109-111, 115-117; trans. by Henry Wadsworth
Longfellow)

Part of what the atheists have rejected is precisely the kind of idle speculation that they hear from the pulpits, twaddle that causes any nascent faith they might have had to be put to the test.

Other reasons also abound for rejection of the Creed. The 20th century saw this denial of the truths expressed in the Creed by large numbers of people including those professing scientism (the theory that anything not suitable for scientific verification does not exist) and Communism. Among those who did believe in immaterial realities, the 20thcentury saw many who no longer thought of God as the Father and Creator but more as a divine energy (a simplistic reduction).

Polarities began to develop that brought about a perceived chasm between faith and science as philosophers and theologians rushing to defend the conscious, personal, omnipotent creator God as maker of heaven and earth against the forces of materialist reductivism. In the Catholic Church, what was called Neo-Thomism(through six courses in philosophy taught to all those attending Catholic universities)was able to strengthen believers against the inroads of atheism, agnosticism and, later, against New Age half-truths about the divine. In its zeal for answers, many of those in the 20th Century did not honor the complexity or profundity of that which is real.

Among non-Catholic Christians, the impact, of what was mocked by some as Fundamentalism, on 20th century Protestants was enormous. By the end of the year 2000, attendance at such evangelical churches was greater than that of main-line denominations. "Do you know Jesus as your personal savior?" became the question for evangelists of such churches.

Among non-Christian Abrahamic theists, we find similar shifting back to the roots of the faith. Whereas at the beginning of the 20th century most Jews and many Muslims were modernist in philosophy and non-practitioners of orthodox rituals and rules, by the end of the century there was a revival of orthodox Judaism and a huge growth in Islamic fervor. The growth may be attributed to many factors— including a lack of affirmation of spiritual reality in the world at large.

Catholic teaching, on the other hand, moved away in some places from basic fundamentals to a less catechetical approach, such that some young Catholics could no longer articulate the doctrine of the Trinity. Whereas cradle-Catholics of the first half of the 20th century were taught at Catholic schools or Catechism programs the basic truths found in the Baltimore Catechism including the Creed, by the end of the 20th century we have a different story. After the glorious second Vatican Council, many universities dropped the 6 course Neo-Thomist sequence, instead requiring only 1 or 2 courses in philosophy and theology.

Many writers of catechisms were convinced that older ways of teaching relied too heavily on a rote approach and, therefore, failed to convey the personal love of God so essential for authentic faith. In the process of rewriting the catechism, some experts managed to marginalize belief in specific Catholic teachings to the point where their students no longer could answer such questions as "What does the word Trinity mean?" In essence, the changes—though often motivated by good intention—failed to capture the complex richness of truth. Many teachers misjudged the importance of their own theological and philosophical knowledge and the role it played in cultivated their love of God, their neighbors, and themselves.

During the 20ᵗʰ century, many parish Catholics left the Church over changes such as the use of the vernacular in the liturgy or omission in preaching of teachings essential to the deposit of the faith. Others left the Church precisely because they dissented from specific teachings, especially moral teachings. Without the emphasis on hell that characterized pre-Vatican II preaching, teens and young adults slowly stopped going to Church at all.

Not only is hell real, but it also exists as a kind of beacon—that good and evil exist, that we may know the difference between the two, and that our choices have eternal consequences. To affirm the existence of hell is to affirm part of reality. Viewing God not so much as "the Father Almighty" but more as a source of unconditional love, they thought the "rules" of the Church to be old-fashioned. We have lost some commons sense: that what is real is always real—and the source of all reality, God, is oldest of all. Many 20ᵗʰ century orthodox thinkers—such as G. K. Chesterton, C. S. Lewis, and Peter Kreeft—have made it clear that we cannot tell what is true or not by how old it is or how new it is.

What would Catholic Realism look like?

Some polarities affirm an absence, both in the world and in the Church, and an adequate response might be a synthesis, which is the current project of Catholic Realism. What would it look like? First, it would restore a study of the Catechism as foundational to an understanding of the faith articulated by the Creed, and it would advance the Deposit of the Faith as found in Scripture and Tradition through the Magisterium as its proper steward.

It would then demonstrate through science itself that a position of material reductivism is not tenable. It would enlighten Catholic students with books by scientists who were convinced that God existed precisely because of scientific facts and theories. As we proceed into the 21st century, more and more texts and courses are being created today on how to refute atheism, and theymake use of the writings of scientists. It is sound to view science and faith as partners, not as enemies, as they describe one reality.

On the other side of the spectrum, how do New Age ideas influence our thinking about what exits? Of course, God is not an impersonal divine energy permeating but not creating the universe. At the same time, contemporary Catholic evangelists do well to listen to the experience of those who often left our Church to enter into New Age explorations so to build a bridge to them. A convert godson and a close friend of Dr. Chervin's were New-Agers who found the fulfillment of what they sought in popular New Age spiritualities in the God of the Creed.

What about the 21st century Catholic character and the concept of God? Dr. Chervin puts it this way: "I never want to hear again a statement of a student in 1969 who defined God simply as 'The one who can zap me out of existence!' Does that sound like God the Father?" On the other hand, neither does she want to hear God defined as "the Father in heaven who loves me so much that He will never judge me no matter what I do." If we are not careful, we may be lead into a belief that negates an essential reality in order to escape another belief and its baggage that is problematic because it denies an essential reality: *out of the pot but into the fire.*

As much work as there is to do in converting the world to Christ, the first conversion experience of any dialogue lies with ourselves, in a transformation of our capacities to love one another and see Christ even within those who do not see him within themselves. We must seek our own continued conversion in Christ in order to offer Christ to others. To this end, the Pontifical Council for Inter-Religious Dialogue speaks in its document "Dialogue and Proclamation" (1991) of four kinds of dialogue:

> *a)* The *dialogue of life,* where people strive to live in an open and neighbourly spirit, sharing their joys and sorrows, their human problems and preoccupations.
> *b)* The *dialogue of action,* in which Christians and others collaborate for the integral development and liberation of people.
> *c)* The *dialogue of theological exchange,* where specialists seek to deepen their understanding of their respective religious heritages, and to appreciate each other's spiritual values.
> *d)* The *dialogue of religious experience,* where persons, rooted in their own religious traditions, share their spiritual riches, for instance with regard to prayer and contemplation, faith and ways of searching for God or the Absolute. (42)

The document speaks of these four kinds of dialogue not as discrete methods but as an interconnected reality. "Contacts in daily life and common commitment to action will normally open the door for cooperation in promoting human and spiritual values," the document explains. "[T]hey may also eventually lead to the dialogue of religious experience in response to the great questions which the circumstances of life do not fail to arouse in the minds of people," such as sensing the spiritual presence of our beloved dead. In addition, "Exchanges at the level of religious experience can give more life to theological discussions. These in turn can enlighten experience and encourage closer contacts." In the case of atheism, non-belief itself forms a kind of belief-system, and it is within that system that we find room for dialogue.

To approach dialogue with atheism in such a way as to increase understanding and enrich relationships, one must first enter into an authentic relationship with atheists through an understanding of this belief-system and its traditions. While the varieties of atheism differ according to their traditions, the essence of atheism entails a common profession: there being no supernatural cause. Atheism, which by its nature is materially reductive, contains within it, then, ultimately no hope for eternal happiness because of the belief that the soul, if it exists as even an animating force, perishes with the body.

This would even seem to affect natural happiness, for, as St. Augustine writes to God in Book I of his *Confessions*, "You move us to delight in praising You; for You have formed us for Yourself, and *our hearts are restless till they find rest in You*" (italics mine). That lack of belief in an immortal soul in itself then speaks to a "belief-tradition." Our encounter with that belief-tradition is the starting point of our dialogue, for it gives us an opportunity to demonstrate an awareness of the faith we are addressing if not also of the person(s) with whom we are speaking.

When we do enter into dialogue with atheists, it happens not only because of our awareness of the belief-system of the atheists, but also because of our awareness of our own faith tradition--for no true dialogue exists between partners unequally versed in the essential elements about which they are speaking. We Catholics--or, more broadly, we Christians—must know ourselves before we can authentically engage another, and we must know atheism sufficiently to understand the terms on which we would most naturally be using equivocally. Seeking dialogue understand that we understand our own tradition and that of another person.

As *"Dialogue and Proclamation"* professes, "Far from weakening [our Christian] faith, true dialogue will deepen it. [Christians] will become increasingly aware of their Christian identity and perceive more clearly the distinctive elements of the Christian message" (50). In this way, we can stand like Christ before the woman at the well and offer her water that will forever slake her thirst, only we might not expect the same quick conversion except through our sustained demonstrations that we ourselves do not thirst. We must demonstrate that the living water has changed us having been given to us by Christ.

The Nature of Inculturation and Evangelization

The *Catechism of the Catholic Church* explains that evangelization "must involve a process of inculturation if the Gospel is to take flesh in each people's culture,"[3] and this implies a "respectful dialogue with those who do not yet accept the Gospel."[4] While the purpose of such a dialogue is the act of proclamation of the Gospel message, the process is not, of course, aimed at proselytizing, for a more fruitful exchange and authentic encounter will be had without it. Instead of trusting to outward pressure for some hoped for goal of conversion, we trust, instead, to conversion through the dynamic internal change of truth and love objectively understood—from God working from the inside out.

---

[3] Catechism of the Catholic Church, 2nd ed. (Washington, DC: United States Catholic Conference, 2000), 854. Three sound-alike words ending in "culturation" are as follows: Inculturation is the process of finding the Gospel message as it is currently being lived among an uncatechized people and drawing out the fullness of the Gospel from that standpoint, such as the missionary's demonstration that the brotherly love shown among tribes has its origin in a common Creator. Acculturation, on the other hand, is a means by which to replace a minority culture with the dominant culture, such as efforts to eradicate home language in favor of dominant language. Enculturation is a means by which to nurture those who are already members of a culture.

[4] Catechism of the Catholic Church, 856.

Inculturation

The essence of inculturation is the appropriate adaptation of the Gospel message to the community within which it is being preached, resulting in the incarnation of the message "in the culture and the spiritual tradition of those addressed, so that the message is not only intelligible to them, but is conceived as responding to their deepest aspirations, as truly the Good News they have been longing for."[5] Evangelization would be forced, otherwise, and result in a form of proselytism that denies the rights of the Other to freely embrace Christianity. *Dignitatis humanae* is rather emphatic on the necessity to distinguish between evangelization and proselytism in its assertion that

> in spreading religious faith and in introducing religious practices everyone ought at all times to refrain from any manner of action which might seem to carry a hint of coercion or of a kind of persuasion that would be dishonorable or unworthy, especially when dealing with poor or uneducated people. Such a manner of action would have to be considered an abuse of one's right [to preach] and a violation of the right of others.[6]

---

[5] Pontifical Council for Interreligious Dialogue, *Dialogue and Proclamation:* Reflection and Orientations on Interreligious Dialogue and the Proclamation of the Gospel of Jesus Christ (19 May 1991), § 70. Online 30 November, 2009, at http://www.vatican.va/roman_curia/pontifical_councils/interelg/documents/rc_pc_interelg_doc_19051991_dialogue-and-proclamatio_en.html.

[6] Paul VI, Declaration on Religious Freedom *Dignitatis humanae* on the Right of the Person and of Communities to Social and Civil Freedom in Matters Religious (7 December 1965), § 4. Online December 8, 2009, at

The missionary endeavor, consequently, requires patience to work within a different set of cultural values. To enter into the possibility of realizing the fruits of authentic dialogue, the Catholic has to study not only his own faith but also the belief-system of the atheist.

Our understanding this belief-system is what enables an authentic process of inculturation, which is the process through which dialogue and proclamation are enacted so that the Gospel message may be revealed within any non-Christian community. It is ontologically grounded, with recognition of the Truth on the part of the Catholic, but is epistemologically expressed, through finding opportunities to engage the atheist community in general and the atheist-in-front-of-you in particular in the kind of dialogue that allows us to proclaim without coercion the fullness of faith in Christ.

Because it is a dialogue, the Catholic cannot expect to impose his or her own agenda at every encounter but be open to a greater understanding of the belief-system of the atheist to whom he or she is proclaiming the truth of Christ. That openness will not only facilitate the discussion, but it will likely provide opportunities for further explication of the Catholic faith. Pope Benedict XVI, writing when he was Cardinal Ratzinger, explained in *Dominus Iesus* that the Church,

> guided by charity and respect for freedom, must be primarily committed to proclaiming to all people the truth definitively revealed by the Lord, and to announcing the necessity of conversion to Jesus Christ and of adherence to the Church through Baptism and the other sacraments, in order to participate fully in

http://www.vatican.va/archive/hist_councils/ii_vatican_council/doc uments/vat-ii_decl_19651207_dignitatis-humanae_en.html.

communion with God, the Father, Son and Holy Spirit.[7]

The charity and respect for freedom that guides this kind of a conversation will lead the atheist to understand that being Christian is a fuller expression of his or her belief system, which terminates with man without satisfactorily answering the question of the cause of man except in evolutionary terms that fall into infinite regress. All men, Aristotle writes in his *Metaphysics*, desire to know, so we all pursue the truth, even though some of us stop short of our goal whenever we think we have found it. The atheist is dealing with only a partial truth – that man exists and has a mind capable of acting upon the world – but lacks the fullness of truth, that man's existence is contingent on a necessary being who not only created him but also seeks a personal relationship with him. The authenticity of our own faith relationship with God is a reality that must not be absent to dialogue.

Because so many people stop short of realizing the Truth in spite of their quest for it, we Catholics, who have the Truth, are obliged to share it with them. This obligation is a part of our teaching apostolate, and all Catholics should learn their faith sufficiently to be able to carry it out. According to the *Catechism*, we "proclaim the Good News to those who do not know it, in order to consolidate, complete, and raise up the truth and the goodness that God has distributed among men and nations, and to purify them from error and evil."[8] That error and evil lies in the denial of Christ's divinity precisely because it is a denial of the true nature of God who is

---

[7] Joseph Cardinal Ratzinger, Declaration *Dominus Iesus* on the Unicity and Salvific Universality of Jesus Christ and the Church, Congregation for the Doctrine of the Faith (6 August 2000), § 22. Online 23 November, 2009, at http://www.vatican.va/roman_curia/congregations/cfaith/documents/rc_con_cfaith_doc_20000806_dominus-iesus_en.html.

[8] Catechism of the Catholic Church, 856.

relationship and who became incarnate to us in a special act of inculturation in order to reveal to us our true selves. Christ entered into our world and offers to raise us up in Him. Christ offers to unfold the meaning of life for us.

For this reason, the obligation we have to proclaim the good news of Christ necessarily reaches beyond the surface.

> What matters is to evangelize man's culture and cultures (not in a purely decorative way, as it were, by applying a thin veneer, but in a vital way, in depth and right to their very roots), in the wide and rich sense which these terms have in *Gaudium et spes*, always taking the person as one's starting-point and always coming back to the relationships of people among themselves and with God.[9]

We get to that starting point by first coming to know the person with whom we are starting. Knowing the person is the beginning. We cannot do it by simply dropping in on him or her and blowing the equivalent of the theological horn in his or her ear.

When we approach the atheist, then we do so from an understanding of the equality in personal dignity they share with us as a consequence of their being human persons. That is to say, they are also "beings endowed with reason and free will and therefore privileged to bear personal responsibility,"[10] within whom the Holy Spirit may reside. An understanding of basic catechetical methods can assist us in our work:

---

[9] Paul VI, *Evangelii nuntiandi*, Apostolic Exhortation (8 December 1975), § 20. Online December 8, 2009, at http://www.vatican.va/holy_father/paul_vi/apost_exhortations/documents/hf_p-vi_exh_19751208_evangelii-nuntiandi_en.html.
[10] *Dignitatis humanae*, § 2.

We can say of catechesis, as well as of evangelization in general, that it is called to bring the power of the Gospel into the very heart of culture and cultures. For this purpose, catechesis will seek to know these cultures and their essential components; it will learn their most significant expressions; it will respect their particular values and riches. In this manner it will be able to offer these cultures the knowledge of the hidden mystery and help them to bring forth from their own living tradition original expressions of Christian life, celebration and thought.[11]

The incarnation of the Truth brought forth in such a way is the heart of inculturation, for it enables the proclamation of the Word to make equals in doctrine persons who are already equals in dignity. *Dominus Iesus* explains the meaning of this idea of equality as "a presupposition of inter-religious dialogue, [which] refers to the equal personal dignity of the parties in dialogue, not to doctrinal content, nor even less to the position of Jesus Christ - who is God himself made man - in relation to the founders of the other religions."[12] Because we know that the doctrinal content that is proclaimed throughout our dialogue is different from that to which the atheists adhere, and this is primarily understood from their rejection of a supernatural cause, we must also know that it will be their greatest point of resistance when confronted with it.

As Catholics proclaiming the faith to those who already have experienced resistance, we want to develop structures that enable us to work within the grain of that resistance rather than against it. It is, once more, "one of the major tenets

---

[11] John Paul II, *Catechesi tradendae*, Apostolic Exhortation (16 October 1979), § 53. Online December 7, 2009, at http://www.vatican.va/holy_father/john_paul_ii/apost_exhortations /documents/hf_jp-ii_exh_16101979_catechesi-tradendae_en.html.
[12] *Dominus Iesus*, § 22.

49 | C a t h o l i c   R e a l i s m :   a   F r a m e w o r k   f o r   t h e
R e f u t a t i o n   o f   A t h e i s m   a n d   t h e   E v a n g e l i z a t i o n
o f   A t h e i s t s

of Catholic doctrine that man's response to God in faith must be free: no one therefore is to be forced to embrace the Christian faith against his own will."[13] It is through this means that we achieve authenticity in our relationship with those with whom we are in dialogue, for without authenticity we have no substantial basis for any dialogue. Without honoring the free will and dignity of persons, we cannot have true dialogue.

Authenticity in any relationship merely means that one represents oneself as one is rather than endeavoring to pass oneself off as something that one is not. One's belonging to a particular faith tradition, then, becomes part of the conversation when one encounters someone from a different belief-system for the purposes of discussing matters concerning their belief.

Such is the nature of these commonalities that it is also obvious to us, to quote a favorite maxim of our Popes since Blessed Paul VI, that what unites us is far greater than what divides us, and that is a realization that fosters a great deal of hope in the fruitfulness of the exchange.

Practical Applications

Dialogue is the path to the goal of proclamation. The effort of our dialoguing as a means for proclamation is the thing to which we want to habituate ourselves in our own ministries. We cannot have true proclamation without authentic dialogue.

As "Proclamation and Dialogue" explains, these two words are "both viewed, each in its own place, as component elements and authentic forms of the one evangelizing mission of the Church. They are both oriented towards the communication of salvific truth." That is to say, according to a

---

[13] *Dignitatis humanae*, § 10.

letter to the Presidents of Bishops Conferences on the Spirituality of Dialogue written on March 3, 1999, "In dialogue the Christian is called to be a witness to Christ, imitating the Lord in his proclamation of the Kingdom, his concern and compassion for each individual person and his respect for that person's liberty."

In short, then, the purpose of dialogue is proclamation, but since we cannot force conversion we ought to pursue sustainability in our interactions with others so that, over time, they can come to see the true light of Christ within us and be drawn toward it by their own inherent impulses toward God. We must subordinate our hopes to the work that God is doing in each of us. It is vital, too, that we understand the obstacles that we ourselves will be to the process. Obstacles to this goal of authentic dialogue exist on our part, namely the following:

a) Insufficient grounding in one's own faith.
b) Insufficient knowledge and understanding of the belief and practices of other religions, leading to a lack of appreciation for their significance and even at times to misrepresentation.
c) Socio-political factors or some burdens of the past.
d) Wrong understanding of the meaning of terms such as conversion, baptism, dialogue, etc.
e) Self-sufficiency, lack of openness leading to defensive or aggressive attitudes.
f) A lack of conviction with regard to the value of interreligious dialogue, which some may see as a task reserved to specialists, and others as a sign of weakness or even a betrayal of the faith.
g) Suspicion about the other's motives in dialogue.
h) A polemical spirit when expressing religious convictions.

i) Intolerance, which is often aggravated by association with political, economic, racial and ethnic factors, a lack, of reciprocity in dialogue which can lead to frustration.

j) Certain features of the present religious climate, e.g., growing materialism, religious indifference, and the multiplication of religious sects which creates confusion and raises new problems. [14]

If we Catholics can invest the time in removing some of these obstacles, and many are easily removed with appropriate instruction in the areas of study, prayer, and fasting, then our own efforts at authentically encountering the atheistic worldview will be fruitful. The Council has explained that the manner in which Christians will respond to the call to personal involvement in dialogue and proclamation "will depend on the circumstances and also on their degree of preparation,"[15] which is something we Catholics ought to take as a challenge to prepare not only ourselves but also our children for the work that lies ahead of us.

That work is grounded in the reality of human diversity and plurality of belief. Cardinal Arinze, on the January 24, 2002, day of prayer at Assisi, wrote,

> This plurality is a fact. People have to learn to accept it. Positive efforts have to continue to promote better mutual understanding and greater collaboration between people of differing religions or cultural backgrounds. Cultures and religions can collide. But they need not collide. Such a clash can be avoided. Indeed, humanity should go beyond avoiding a clash and promote harmony and collaboration.

---

[14] *Dialogue and Proclamation*, § 52.
[15] *Dialogue and Proclamation*, § 82.

That we might work toward harmony and collaboration with non-theists qua their non-theism with perhaps no realization of success in their conversion does not mean that we cease to proclaim God or reveal God in our lives during our interactions with them. One of the things that impressed the pagans so much during the early days of the Church, after all, was the witness of how well the Christians loved one another. Our demonstrating that kind of love makes our faith attractive as will be shown by so many atheists such as Dr. Chervin herself who discovered the fullness of life—of joy in God-- expressed best in our Catholic theism.

A catechist who teaches only Catholics in his or her home parish, furthermore, is as engaged in the work of evangelizing the future generations of atheists as the catechist who is pursuing dialogue in the larger public forum. After all, as Yves Congar has written, the proper focus of ecclesiology is the local community. Because "[i]nculturation must involve the whole People of God, and not just a few experts,"[16] the challenge lies open to all of us to enter into this dialogue for the sake of proclamation. The souls we encounter in the beatific vision might praise God's beneficence that he cared enough to send missionaries imbued with the Holy Spirit who were able to more fully reveal to them the truth of Christ to which their atheism had blinded them. To see Christ is to see the foundations of the world—and of all joy.

---

[16] General Directory for Catechesis, 206.

Chapter 2: Types of Atheists and Stories of Converts
by Dr. Ronda Chervin

When people think of the history of atheism, they often have in mind those who thought that Darwin proved we do not need a God to explain the universe. Whether scientists such as Darwin were atheists themselves is somewhat controversial. In the 19th century there could still be societal penalties for being a professed atheist. Some historians, consequently, insist that many professed agnostics (those who claim that we cannot know whether there is a God or not given our limited minds) and even those who sometimes attended religious services were likely hidden atheists.

Scientifically-based atheism, however, is only one type of atheism. Others include literary atheism, Communist atheism, philosophical types of atheism from Russell to Sartre, psychologically based atheism, and New Age substitution of the concept of some sort of energy for a personal God of Love. And, of course, there is much overlap between the different types. (Rejection of a God who allows suffering—which, ironically, is a form of rejection of a God who is unjust—will be dealt with in chapter 5.) In the pages that follow, we will first describe the kinds of atheists and their arguments for their atheism so that that may be understood and their arguments refuted.

Scientifically-based Atheism

Typically, many in the past believed that science itself had eliminated God as an explanation for the existence of the world and of mankind. The fortunes of chance replaced an intelligent Creator. Atheism pushed out theism by stating that theism only flourished because pre-scientific minds had no other explanation for the beings around them. The evolution of religion from primitive polytheism to monotheism was regarded as one kind of evolutionary step that would lead to the gradual elimination of any personal deity. The universe itself came to be seen by atheists influenced by science as self-sufficient with no beginning or end—an endless series And when physicists became convinced there would be an end to the universe, that theory was not held by atheists to prove that there was also a beginning, requiring a Creator God. Principles of coherence and correspondence were sacrificed at the altar of Evolution.

Regarding the so-called transition from primitive polytheism to monotheism, some anthropologists personally investigated primitive tribes in remote places where no missionaries had ever been to influence them, and found that such primitives were essentially monotheistic. As well as having "little gods" they had one creator God. There is a famous 12-volume work on this subject by Wilhelm Schmidt on the Origin of the Idea of God.[17] Such researchers believe that all food-gathering primitives are monotheistic in this sense and that polytheism became widespread with the beginning of towns.

Such scientific atheism was so prevalent among atheists when I was growing up that I never conceived that there could even be a scientist who was also religious! In preparation for teaching the philosophy of God many years later, I was astounded to read about well-known scientists who insisted there was a God. Here are some quotations from their writings.

---

[17] Wilhelm Schmidt, *The Origin and Growth of Religion; Facts and Theories* (New York: Cooper Square Publishers, 1972).

With regard to the view that we do not need God to cause the universe which was always here with no beginning), astronomer Robert Jastrow reports that there is evidence that the universe came into existence abruptly and this description corresponds to the Biblical view:

> The evidence lies in the fact that all the galaxies – the great cluster of stars that populate the heavens – are moving away from us and one another at enormous speeds, as if they were recoiling from the scene of a great explosion. If the motions of the outward-moving galaxies are traced backwards in time, we find that they all come together, so to speak, about 20 billion years ago. At that time all the matter in the Universe was packed into one dense mass under enormous pressure and with temperatures ranging up to trillions of degrees. The picture suggests the explosion of a cosmic hydrogen bomb. The instant in which the cosmic bomb exploded marked the birth of the universe.[18]

And the potential of its birth has unfolded to this very moment.

As to whether the universe as we know it exhibits contingency—that it is dependent on a being outside of itself—physicist Stanley L. Jaki writes, "Einstein's theories really lead away from the idea of an infinite universe as a reason not to need God. Instead, they lead us toward the image of a specific universe. This specificity, signifies contingency, dependence on something else."[19]

---

[18] Roy Abraham Varghese, *The Intellectuals Speak Out About God: a Handbook for the Christian Student in a Secular Society.* (Chicago: Regnery, 1984), 15.

[19] Varghese, *The Intellectuals Speak Out About God*, 61.

In *The New Story of Science* by Augros and Stancui, we find a discussion of the overarching issue about scientific atheism which is called *scientism*. This is a term used by theists to critique a basic assumption of those who base their atheism on science. Scientism is defined as the conviction that the methods of science are the only reliable ways to secure knowledge of anything—that science is the whole truth about reality. The problem with scientism is that it cuts off the branch upon which it rests from the tree upon which it depends.

After I became a believer I used to humorously ask atheistic boyfriends if they could use science as a way to prove they loved me. If not, then why should I not believe them when they said they loved me? Behind this "joke" is the truth that all kinds of things are outside the range of science such as love, beauty, and, especially, truth. Deciding that something is true or false is an act of the immaterial intellect. Science itself cannot prove that scientific method is the only way to know. If science is not the only source of truth, then it follows there could be other sources of truth about the origin of the universe, such as philosophical arguments about the universe not being always just there, but needing a cause outside itself. There will be much more about scientifically based atheism in Dr. Mahfood's "Chapter 4: Science and Theism."

Literary Atheism

By literary atheism I mean doubts about God's existence or convictions about His non-existence expressed by fictional characters. Such fictional atheists exerted a powerful influence over intellectuals, especially in Europe in the 19th century. I am thinking of the famous proclamation in Nietzsche famous book *Thus Spake Zarathustra* that "God is Dead." Now Nietzsche, originally a philologist, then a philosopher, and then a fiction writer, did not mean that there once really was a God, an absolute perfect, omniscient, omnipotent, personal God who one day up and died!

No, "God is dead" was a literary image expressing the fact that the imaginary God of the Bible and of Judeo-Christian culture was no longer necessary. Human beings would do better dispensing with the notion of God and, in His peace, becoming themselves supermen and superwomen. The fantastical, mythical Zarathustra of Nietzsche's sensational book was the herald of the brilliant, courageous, bold, defiant, and creative new men and women who would usher forth from the demise of the Christian archetype of mankind with its insistence, according to Nietzsche, on making people into miserable meek, subservient, docile, pseudo-saints.

Now, neither of my parents read Nietzsche. But his ideas permeated the early 20th century. In particular, Nietzsche called not for some kind of despairing atheism, but for a joyful liberation from the shackles of traditional religion. The fear most people had that death check-mated any joy in life unless there was an after-life, Nietzsche tried to conquer by means of a theory that after death, thousands of years afterwards, the entire universe comes back with everything the same again, including each of us. This was called eternal recurrence. A bi-product of the Nietzschean-styled joyful atheism of my parents is that we, their children, were not allowed ever to be sad. Showing anxiety or despair could call up the need for a divine redeemer. But, since they did not believe in Nietzsche's eternal recurrence theory, when they actually faced death each of them, in their own way, did reach out to God.

An indication of the undying fame of Nietzsche's phrase "God is dead" is this graffiti I saw on the walls of the New York subway:

"God is dead." Nietzsche
"Nietzsche is dead." God

The end of a being points to its finite nature. Christ's resurrection points to His eternal nature.

Another literary account of atheism written in the 19th century, but well-known in the United States in the 20th century, is that of Leo Tolstoy (who I believe to have been one of the greatest novelists of all time). In the book, *Anna Karenina*, Tolstoy himself an ardent Christian, depicts a highly sensitive and virtuous man, Levin, plagued by doubts of God's existence. This character displays all the reasonings Tolstoy himself suffered through in the case of his own conversion. He is saved from suicidal despair by God's grace and becomes a holy family man.

In a more convoluted intellectual manner, Dostoevsky's character, Ivan, in the famous *Brothers Karamazov,* represents atheism springing from disgust with the way man victimizes man. Ivan compiles accounts from the newspapers of hideous crimes against humanity such as parents locking a little child in the outhouse for days because she wets her bed. He concludes that it is better not to believe in a God who could allow such things to happen.

To the argument that in heaven all the tears of victims are dried and their broken hearts consoled, Ivan retorts that if such a heaven exists he would rather go to hell than accept it as a reward for tolerating such evils. The saintly monk hero of the same book, Zossima, claims that the remedy for atheism is not arguments but simply love. If the skeptic would spend his or her time only being loving, the doubts would gradually be dissolved as human love reflected God's love.

A much admired woman fiction writer, Ayn Rand, develops an atheism of a different flavor. The heroine of one of her novels, *Atlas Shrugged,* is a brilliant, resourceful, railroad executive, Dagny. She rebels against the cowardly, dishonest practices of the business world of the United States between the two World Wars. Religion is rarely mentioned except as a part of the weak conformism of those who are willing to sell themselves out to win money and approval from others.

A less toxic kind of literary atheism I find in some contemporary books is manifested through religious characters who are depicted as following traditions only as traditions, not as real encounters with a living God even though the language of these characters reflects real belief. The authors' description of any religious service is patronizing, as if to say – part of the decorations of the personalities of my heroes and heroines is the faith they hold to. Emphasis is on how other characters in the book can be ethical without religious beliefs. Such atheist writers never confront believers, since they think faith to be comforting to weak or undereducated people. They patronize them and choose arguments against theism that oversimplify the diverse roots for the goodness of their characters.

Philosophical Atheism

19th and 20th century philosophical atheism took many forms. The most popular, coming out of Logical Positivism and most Analytic philosophy, was to consider that nothing can be meaningful unless it can be verified in a scientific manner. Here is a little sample of reasoning in analytic philosophy that springs from atheism, in this case involving the immaterial part of the human person. Gilbert Ryle developed the following analogy to explain why there is no soul, only a body.[20] Consider someone from a primitive tribe who never heard of or visited a university. He is shown first the administration building, then the gym, then the science building, etc. After that he says, "well, I saw these places, now where is the university." According to Ryle he is making a

---

[20] Gilbert Ryle. *The Concept of Mind* (New University of Chicago Press ed. Chicago: University of Chicago Press, 2002).

category mistake. He thinks the university is an entity separate from its parts. In a similar way, someone who believes in the soul thinks the soul is something other than the legs moving, the heart beating and the brain cells operating. The word *soul* is just a word for the whole living body. Yet Ryle makes a kind of dimensional mistake: for the purpose of the university is the development of persons ordered to their own good, the common good, and to their end—the spirit of a good university makes the difference in whether or not all of the buildings have a reason for being. Perhaps Ryle misunderstood the primitive's question due to his lack of imagination; perhaps the primitive was asking how the university was ordered to the soul's good?

You can see how such thinkers don't believe that "God" is a meaningful term. It is just an old word related to religion before people realized we don't need an explanation for the universe at all. This way of think betrays an absence of understanding of history, at the very least. Human history is filled with ages and civilizations that did certain things well; each generation tends to have strengths and weaknesses different from those which preceded it.

Most prominent in debates about God was Bertrand Russell. Brought up as a Christian, he would come to the conviction that the only things we can be sure even exist are those that can be known through the senses. Accordingly God, being by definition non-sensate, could not be proven or disproven. Among Russell's peers, God and the soul were considered mere figments of the imagination. It was thought that the only future for philosophers was to give up speculating about the meaning of the life and the universe and confine themselves to engendering criteria for evaluating scientific theories or problems stemming from language.

Quite different is the atheism of some 20th century existentialists. Not all existentialists are atheists. The first philosopher to invent the term was Kierkegaard, a staunch

Danish Lutheran. Existentialism was at first a reaction against wild metaphysical speculations, especially those of Hegel. Instead of thinking about abstractions such as being and becoming, philosophers need to be helping their followers to get insight into their life choices. An example, for Kierkegaard, would be analyzing the choices in life between pleasure-seeking (including being an intellectual dilettante instead of a lover of truth), commitment to ethical goodness, and surrender to God. One of Kierkegaard's wittiest comments regarding atheism was this: "Presumably God waits in the lobby while the academics in the classroom decide if He exists or not." Another comment equally incisive is this one: "There is a Copernican revolution in the heart of a man when he realizes it is not he who judges God but God who judges him."

The most influential existential atheist was Jean Paul Sartre. Brought up in a Catholic home by doting female relatives, Sartre admits that he began to hate God when he realized that he could easily get his way with those relatives but that with God that was impossible. This he realized when hiding in the bathroom burning something for fun. God could see him even though his aunts could not.

Sartre's intellectual argument for the non-existence of God was developed in his masterpiece *Being and Nothingness*. [21] There Sartre distinguishes two kinds of being – the in-itself and the for-itself. The in-itself includes everything of matter which lacks consciousness and freedom. The for-itself is what humans are because our essence is to be free. The in-itself is opaque. The for-itself is open. Now these two types of being are contradictions. But the traditional absolute personal God is supposed to combine both types of being. That God is supposed to be totally free yet absolute and unchanging.

---

[21] Jean Paul Sartre, *Being and Nothingness: a Phenomenological Essay On Ontology* (New York: Pocket Books, 1978).

Therefore, there can be no such God—so goes Sartre's argument

Many followers of Sartre became despairing drop outs. Sartre did not approve of this. He maintained that one must make choices in life and not try to become an in-itself by becoming a corpse instead of a person. He thought that we could understand the lack of authenticity of bad actions without religion.

Interestingly enough, I learned from someone who appeared to be in a position to know that when near to his death Sartre secretly sent for a priest to be reconciled to the Church. He kept this secret because his followers said they would abandon him if this betrayal of his atheism became public. It is said that Sartre quipped that he was the 6th proof for the existence of God because he was so important to 20th century thought that God had to invent him!

More of an agnostic, and later in life possibly a believer, was the French existentialist and novelist Albert Camus. In *The Plague,* he depicts a modern city in North Africa afflicted with a plague.[22] His hero is a doctor, who is an atheist, whose compassion leads him to empty himself out in service to the victims. This doctor is Camus' model of sacrifice without religious belief. The contrasting figure is the priest who castigates the people for their sins and mediocrity he believes to have brought down God's wrath upon them. Partly because of his contact at the death beds of victims where he comes to know the atheist doctor, this priest eventually tries to give spiritual help to the victims leaving as a mystery why God has allowed this suffering.

There is a book written by a French Protestant minister narrating how before Camus died in a car accident, possibly a

---

[22] Albert Camus, *The Plague*, 1st Vintage international ed. (New York: Vintage, 1991).

suicide, that this famous writer used to visit the Christian Church looking for hope and answers.

Communist Atheism

It is the 19th century Karl Marx who coined the phrase that "religion is the opiate of the people."[23] Mankind is oppressed by many political, economic and social factors, so because people can see no way out, they dream of a heaven where all will be well and then resign themselves to being victims. Instead they need to throw off religion and fight for the betterment of their life on earth. Basically "God" is seen as a rival to man who must destroy religion in order to become as great as he can be.

Marx was the son of Jew who became Lutheran for political reasons. He was not brought up either Christian or Jewish and is thought by some scholars to have been an atheist from youth. Communists do not focus on metaphysical reasons for disbelief in God. They rather take the non-existence of God for granted as a corollary of materialism and concentrate more on dethroning religion as an obstacle to progress.

The phrase used by New York City communists when my parents were in the party to describe this type of atheism was "you'll have pie in the sky when you die." This was a sarcastic description of how religion lures people away from protesting injustice by means of the communist revolution, because they dwell on the joys of heaven instead of fighting for their rights on earth.

Of Communist atheists, those who atheism had the greatest effect on the world were Stalin and Mao Tse-Tung.

---

[23] Karl Marx and Arnold Ruge. *Deutsch-FranzoÌ^sische JahrbuÌ^cher: 1844.* (Leipzig: Reclam, 1981).

Joseph Stalin (1879-1953)

Stalin "was born into a dysfunctional family in a poor village in Georgia (in Russia). Sent by his mother to the seminary in Tiflis (now Tbilisi) to study to become a priest, the young Stalin never completed his education, and was instead soon completely drawn into the city's active revolutionary circles.

> Never a fiery intellectual polemicist or orator like Lenin or Trotsky, Stalin specialized in the humdrum nuts and bolts of revolutionary activity, risking arrest every day by helping organize workers, distributing illegal literature, and robbing trains to support the cause, while Lenin and his bookish friends lived safely abroad and wrote clever articles about the plight of the Russian working class.... In 1922, Stalin was appointed as General Secretary of the Communist Party's Central Committee.
> After Lenin's death in 1924, Stalin methodically went about destroying all the old leaders of the Party... At first, these people were removed from their posts and exiled abroad. Later, when he realized that their sharp tongues and pens were still capable of inveighing against him even from far away, Stalin switched tactics, culminating in a vast reign of terror and spectacular show trials in the 1930s during which the founding fathers of the Soviet Union were one by one unmasked as "enemies of the people" who had supposedly always been in the employ of Capitalist intelligence services and summarily shot.[24]

It is estimated that he had put to death, in one way or another, from twenty to fifty million people!

---

[24] "Joseph Stalin," Red Files, PBS, Available online at http://www.pbs.org/redfiles/bios/all_bio_joseph_stalin.htm

Mao Tse-Tung (1893-1976)

Mao Tse-Tung described by biographer Dick Wilson as a peasant boy climbing by grim determination to become ruler of a great nation.[25] Mao's mother was a devout Buddhist. His father was a non-believer. His father was mean but enterprising. His father moved up from small farmer to big farmer and then to become a trader. At age thirteen, Mao was forced to leave school to work on farm. In his relationship to his father, he learned that if he rebelled he got somewhere but he lost if he was weak and submissive.

Mao desperately wanted a modern education and borrowed from relatives to leave against his father's will. Like Abraham Lincoln, he read in bed with a hidden lamp. Finally, with the money of the relatives, he left home with a mosquito net, two old sheets, a few tunics and 2 books and went to a primary school. He was a rebel in school, gathering the kids together and suggesting that they could retaliate against a mean teacher by killing him!

Mao's first known poem:

To fight with Heaven is infinite pleasure!
To fight with earth is infinite pleasure!
To fight with men is infinite pleasure![26]

At the training school for teachers he attended, Mao read Darwin, Mill, and Rousseau. Pride and anger ruled him. He wrote in his journal, "my boundaries must be expanded so that the universe will become one great self." Mao once told the Dalai Lama that religion is poison and retards progress.

---

[25] Dick Wilson. *The People's Emperor: Mao, a Biography of Mao Tse-tung*, (New York: Lee Publishers Group, arranged with Doubleday & Co., Inc., 1979).

[26] Dick Wilson. *The People's Emperor: Mao, a Biography of Mao Tse-tung* (New York: Doubleday, 1979), p.54.

Later, as a primary school headmaster in a minor provincial city, he became convinced that communism was the only possible instrument for China to cut cleanly through to social justice and economic advance: called the Great Leap Forward and the Cultural Revolution.

Mao himself admitted to the deaths of hundreds of thousands in the course of his introduction of communism after 1949, others say 50 million. Some Chinese said he was the biggest feudal despot in Chinese history. A slogan in the United States during the 1930's was:

> If you're not a communist by the age of 20 you have no heart. If you're still a communist at the age of 30 you have no head.

Psychological Atheism

In the first half of the 20th century, it was Sigmund Freud (1856-1939), brought up in an orthodox Jewish home in Austria, who was the most influential of psychologically based atheists. To the horror of orthodox Jewish rabbis of Europe, Freud, famous as the founder of psycho-analysis, came up with this theory about the origin of belief in God: little children count on their fathers to protect them; then when their father dies or they become old enough to realize that fathers are not omnipotent, they project into the sky a Father-God. This father is the God of the Old Testament. In this way believers avoid feeling as weak, vulnerable and subject to death as they would if they realized there is no God. Of course, the heaven God promises is another aid against fear of death.

A group of prominent rabbis getting wind of the book Freud would soon publish explaining his theory, *Moses and*

Monotheism,[27] came as a delegation to beg him not to let it be printed. He refused to bow to their authority since, as an atheist, he didn't accept the authority of rabbis.

That such a theory influenced so many Jews and people of Christian religions to become, if not atheists, less religious, can easily be explained. Orthodox Judaism in Europe had been abandoned by many in the 19th century due to the Enlightenment. Eager to get out of the ghetto and be enriched by university education, thousands of Jewish young men imbibed the skepticism of such institutions of learning—after all, the ideas worked as levers to further their ambition. If religion could be questioned, then why not remain Jewish but modify the many precepts that kept Jews out of main-line culture? Gradually the Reform Judaism that resulted gave way generation after generation to wide-spread apostasy and an openness to the atheism of Freud.

The argument I like best against Freud's theory, advanced by Karl Stern (1906-1975), a Jewish psychiatrist who became a Catholic,[28] and by Paul Vitz, the famous contemporary teacher of psychology, is this: If you say that God the Father is merely a projection of the human father to assuage fear, equally possible would be that those with authority problems with their fathers, who they can't easily get rid of, instead try to get rid of God by becoming atheists![29]

In Chapter 3 of *Catholic Realism*, we will show how there are absolutely valid proofs for the existence of God. Since this is true, the fact that we might have psychological reasons for wanting there to be a God or not wanting there to be a God

---

[27] Sigmund Freud, *Moses and Monotheism* (New York: Vintage Books, 1939).

[28]Karl Stern. *The Third Revolution* (London: London : M. Joseph, 1955).

[29] Vitz, Paul. *Faith of the Fatherless: The Psychology of Atheism.* (Dallas: Spence Pub. Co., 1999).

makes no difference. We don't think that because some people like rain and others don't that rain doesn't exist!

Some behavioral psychologists such as B.F. Skinner are also atheists. In the case of Skinner, his atheism follows partly from his adoption of the theory of determinism. According to this philosophy, everything we think, feel or do is totally conditioned by previous factors in our lives. If this is true, if there was a God outside our own minds we could never know it because everything in our minds is caused by our programming not by an entity outside our minds. Someone could be an agnostic on this basis, but Skinner, was an atheist before he was a determinist. [30] There are many ways of refuting determinism. A quick way is to ask whether the sentence "determinism is true" is really true or whether someone was just programmed to say that "determinism is true"? If he or she was only programmed, as are all our thoughts according to Skinner, then the theory itself has no independent truth value.

New Age – A Form of Atheism?

The term New Age is a catch-all for many different ideas and practices. From the 1960's onward there was an increasing interest in the West in Eastern spiritualities. By the end of the 20th century, many people left main-line Christian churches to base their interior growth on a variety of methods coming out of the Hindu and Buddhist traditions. Most of those interested in Eastern spirituality were not attracted by the rigors of asceticism of the masters, but more in popularized versions of meditation and fellowship.

---

[30] Skinner, Burrhus Frederic, *The Shaping of a Behaviorist: Part Two of an Autobiography.* (New York: Knopf : distributed by Random House, 1979).

By the 1980's the term New Age became the name for any mixture of astrology, clairvoyance, prophecy, and meditation, with the common theme of breaking away from traditional Christianity into a belief in a cosmic convergence of light. Many New Agers thought that the year 2,000 would bring in radical changes in the universe, perhaps even a unification of intelligences from other planets with our earth's sages.

Often New Agers included in their spiritual synthesis elements of classical Christianity, especially communication with angels, but also with Jesus. The Jesus of most New Agers, however, is different from the Jesus worshiped by Christians in the past. In New Age movements, generally Jesus is seen as only one of the many great sources of light. He is on a par with Buddha, Krishna or with contemporary gurus such as Sai Baba, an alleged worker of miracles in India.

An example of a New Age leader who to tries to bring together the truths of many religions and practices into a synthesis in the Eastern mode but adapted to the West, is Deepak Chopra, an Indian doctor practicing medicine and spirituality primarily in the United States.

Because of the synthetic mode of New Age, it is not always clear that the divine being invoked is not really that same as the personal God of traditional religions. So, one could say that many such New Age ideas and groups are atheistic in not accepting the God of Scripture or of Jewish, Muslim, or Christian philosophy, but are theistic in some sense as wanting to experience the divine in some form.

Because of the ambivalence of much of New Age philosophy and spirituality, I am placing here a summary of the wider differences between classical theistic beliefs and those of many New Agers.

I. Experiential Wisdom vs. Dogmatic Truth

Whereas New Agers hold to individual religious experience even when such is contrary to classical Christian belief, Catholics see their spirituality as a response to the persons of the Trinity and as an exemplification of dogmatic truth.

II. The Divine Within vs. the Transcendent God Within His Creation

Most New Agers think of the Divine as within the soul instead of above and beyond the self. By contrast, Catholics and other believers in revealed religion such as Jews, Moslems and non-Catholic Christians know God as beyond the universe yet being present within it.

III. All is One vs. The Personal Self Reaching Out in Love to God and Other Beings

Many New Agers overcome emotions of loneliness and alienation by immersing themselves in meditative experiences of the oneness of everything in the universe. They seek an ultimate unity where their own selfhood would be fused into the divine. On the contrary, Catholics and others belonging to Western religions believe that the unique self will never disappear since it is created by God in love for the purpose of uniting in love to God, other persons and all other beings of the universe.

IV. Evil Comes from Ignorance vs. Evil Comes from Sin

It is characteristic of many New Age systems of thought to emphasize ignorance as the main source of suffering in the world. An enlightened person chooses good, according to many such New Age philosophies, not so much out of love, but out of desire to avoid the consequences of wrong choices for oneself such as turbulence, anxiety, enslavement. Catholics and others of Judeo-Christian or Moslem background know moral evil and the sufferings which follow to come from the deliberate choice of evil called sin.

V. The Individual is the Final Authority in Spiritual Matters vs. God is the Lord of Our Lives

Many New Agers come from Jewish or Christian families where God was seen as a harsh authority figure, perhaps in the image of their own often unreasonable human fathers. As a result these seekers and others who simply cannot accept traditional religious authority, find comfort in the belief that no one can enforce anything upon them against their own judgment and will. By contrast, Catholics and others coming from a revealed religion will see God's authority as absolutely binding. In a difference of opinion how could the absolute omniscient God be wrong and limited puny-minded I be right?

VI. The Universe is Eternal and the Soul Reincarnated vs. Time has a Beginning and an End and the Soul is Judged by God after one Life

Because many New Agers reject the concept of creation by God at a given moment in time, they tend to think of time in the most common Eastern way as an everlasting cycle. Since they see God as the divine within, there is no God to judge the soul. Instead it evolves from ignorance to enlightenment through a series of incarnations in different bodies. Classical Judeo-Christian thought accepts God's revelation of a beginning and end of time with the soul being judged after one lifetime.

VII: The Best Way to Serve Others is Through Spiritual Teaching vs. Corporal as well as Spiritual Works of Mercy

Generally speaking, most New Agers reject laboring for justice on this earth in terms of righting wrongs or alleviating physical suffering. This is because such seekers think that spiritual solutions are more important. Such a dualistic philosophy is contrary to the Christian insistence that spiritual growth is normally expressed in works of justice and compassion.

Refutations of the ideas of New Agers will be found in Chapter 3 of *Catholic Realism* where you will find proofs for the existence of a personal conscious creator God and proofs for the attributes of God.

The New Atheism

As the above genres have shown, atheism in general is not monolithic. Just as there are many varieties of faith—and the number of those that exist just under the aegis of the Abrahamic religions bears testament to this—there are many varieties of non-faith, or non-belief. They all point, of course, to the same question concerning reality from the viewpoint that there is a God or from the viewpoint that there is no God. This dichotomy understands either that the supernatural world is the form of the natural world designed by an intelligent mind for a meaningful purpose or that there is only the natural world, unformed by anything but chance and without purpose or meaning. The flavors in which these two ideas are expressed are what is varied.

The New Atheism is one such family of flavors, and a chief component of the New Atheism is that it seeks to use scientific demonstration as its principle means of drawing conclusions on the existence of God. The four horseman of the New Atheism who are advancing the idea that the reality of God rests on scientific demonstration alone are Richard Dawkins, Daniel Dennett, Sam Harris, and Christopher Hitchens. They may not be the best advocates for their position, but they are the most popular. Among those who take them to task are Scott Hahn and Benjamin Wiker in their book *Answering the New Atheism: Dismantling Dawkins' Case against God*, Gregory Ganssle in his book *A Reasonable God*, John F. Haught in his book *God and the New Atheism: A Critical Response to Dawkins, Harris, and Hitchens* and Edward Feser in his book *The Last Superstition: A Refutation of the New Atheism.*

According to Feser, the New Atheists are drawing their energy from the idea that the centuries-old "war between science and religion" is now over with the demonstrations of science having clearly defeated the tenets of faith. He points out, like Augros and Stanciu, that the real issue has never been the advances humans have made in the sciences; rather, the real issue has to do with two competing philosophical systems.

What Augros and Stanciu call the Old Story of Enlightenment discoveries of nature's mechanics is really a new story in the grand scheme of things. It explores the mechanics of a purposeless material existence. Feser identifies Descartes as its father. It was out of Cartesian philosophical thinking, along with that of Hobbes, Locke, and Hume who followed him, after all, that this story arose. Descartes, though, didn't intend to limit humankind to a purely material existence, nor did he intend to do away with God. He explains in the preface to his Meditations, a treatise written for the theological faculty at the Sorbonne, that his theory would strengthen religion against the claims of atheism. His splitting the mind and the body was meant to be a philosophical demonstration of the immateriality of the intellect, that even without sensory input the mind would still know that it exists because it is a thinking thing. The Islamic philosopher, Avicenna, had done a similar thought experiment many centuries prior to this in his explanation of the floating man, but Avicenna's ends were different. He was not trying to advance what would become under Descartes a theory of dualism.

The old, old story was philosophical, not scientific, and we find in the philosophical works of Plato, Aristotle, Augustine, and Aquinas a teleological perspective, a perspective that explains what philosophers call a final cause, an end toward which we're directed, a purpose for our being. It's out of this that we get a philosophy of nature, the first philosophical constructs that lead us into an understanding of the natural world, into a method in science. What Augros and Stanciu call the New Story of science, then, is really a return to that older story of philosophy. Where our science has demonstrated a big bang, we find that the scientists also perceive an expanding universe to have had a beginning point from which it is expanding. If that's the case, if both science and religion agree that at some time there was a beginning point, one has to wonder what brought it about, and this is the philosophical question, "Why is there something, and not nothing?"

Questions like this cannot be answered by science because "why" questions are inherently philosophical whenever they ask about the final cause. It's "how" questions that are scientific, that look into the internal mechanics of a thing. They ask about the formal, efficient, and material causes. An acquaintance of mine, Guy Consolmagno, one of the chief astronomers at the Vatican Observatory, has written a book called *God's Mechanics: How Scientists and Engineers Make Sense of Religion*. In it, he explains how scientists, who are trained to be skeptics bent on figuring out how something works, can reconcile science with their faith. After we figure out how something works, I would say, we always want to move to the next step and ask that "why" question. It's akin to the aha-moment – the "okay, I've figured out how the entire universe operates . . . so, hmmm, why is it set up this way? What's its purpose?" The why question is inherently teleological. It resonates with the framework set up by the ancients: we want to know the purpose of things including that of our lives. Any child of the Enlightenment who thinks that there's no purpose to the universe and, like Sartre, can see its existence only as an absurdity, cannot authentically ask the "why" question because it points to a teleological reality that they fundamentally cannot reconcile with their worldview.

Dr. Tom Sheahen, the director of the Institute for Theological Encounter with Science and Technology, often points to a statement he attributes to St. Augustine that the book of nature and the book of revelation are written by the same author, and neither can be in conflict if both are properly understood. Both rely on our reason to understand, and because the defining characteristic of a human person is reason, we're already geared for this study. As rational beings with immaterial intellects, with souls as the form of our bodies, we are called to engage our minds in the study of the natural world precisely because the order of knowledge leads us to an understanding of the order of being.

Philosophically laid out, the order of knowledge is that we come to understand through our senses, which we necessarily apply to the world around us. In so doing, we develop percepts that bring about concepts. For instance, we touch fire and perceive that it's hot, and from that perception, we develop the concept of hotness. We don't need to touch fire again to refresh our minds on what hotness is. Once is enough. That concept of hotness is a universal concept in that many particular things can inhere within it. This ability we have to grasp universals points to a transcendent capacity of the human intellect. We can move in this way along all three levels of philosophical abstraction – the first dealing with material things (within which we work our science), the second dealing with quantifiable things (within which we deal with mathematics), and the third dealing with non-material things (within which we understand metaphysics). Metaphysics, because it concerns non-material being, involves simply the study of being as being.

Aristotle begins his Metaphysics with the simple statement: "All men by nature desire to know." It is in this work that he explains how it is that we come to know – first through our senses, and then through our reason as informed by our senses. The human race, he explains, is different from the other animals in that we live by "art and reasonings." In his encyclical *Fides et Ratio*, Saint John Paul II adds to Aristotle's assertion the very reasonable concept of faith in writing that "Faith and reason are like two wings on which the human spirit rises to the contemplation of truth; and God has placed in the human heart a desire to know the truth—in a word, to know himself—so that, by knowing and loving God, men and women may also come to the fullness of truth about themselves." The fullness of faith cannot be proclaimed without also proclaiming the fullness of reason. They are not only two wings with which we soar, but they are also the two legs on which we take our first steps toward flight. Many of us are hobbling along on one leg or the other, pursuing blind faith or faithless reason.

This brings us back to our definition as humans – that we are rational animals. This adjective "rational" says a great deal about us. It tells us foremost that we are thinkers. It also tells us that our thinking is for some purpose, that purpose necessarily being the pursuit of what is good. We often err by choosing the good-for-my-appetites rather than the good-for-my-being, but that's an issue for moral philosophy, which we'll discuss later. The fact is that we pursue the good because we want happiness. A proximate goal of life is material happiness. An ultimate goal is eternal happiness. Reason tells us that our intellects are immaterial, so they don't die with our bodies. Reason also tells us that our souls are immaterial and are the form of our bodies. Our souls, then, have eternal destinies, and our intellects, that by which we know of our existence and our identity, remain with the form that has its temporal existence in the physical bodies we are using at this very moment.

We do not need faith to know any of this, as Aristotle demonstrated in all the knowledge he advanced without the light of Abrahamic revelation. What faith tells us, though, is far more important. It answers that teleological question that Aristotle struggled with. It answers where these souls go when our material bodies die, namely that they are drawn by love into the beatific vision to live and grow for all eternity in joyful communion with God.

CONVERSIONS FROM ATHEISM TO THEISM

Just as the adage reads "one picture worth a thousand words" I think that "one story is worth a thousand tracts." Why? Maybe because life is more like a story than a syllogism? It is so hard to choose between great stories of converts from atheism to theism. The selection here involved choosing accounts deemed especially likely to interest the readers of this book and a desire to represent diverse national backgrounds.

Jacques Maritain (1882-1973) and Raissa Maritain (1883-1960)[31]: From Atheists to Catholic Philosopher (Jacques) and Mystic (Raissa)

Raissa was born in Russia to a deeply religious Jewish Hasidic family. She and her family migrated to Paris when she was 10 years old. At the Lycée, God began to disappear from her mind, though not from her heart. When Raissa went to the Sorbonne, the students were mostly Darwinists and Marxists, and she, too, came to think that any ideas of God could only be true if science approved of them. While she was studying science, she met Jacques Maritain, her husband-to-be. Jacques was a Parisian whose father was a lawyer, and he had been raised in a liberal Protestant milieu.

Both greatly influenced by Nietzsche, they became atheists. This atheism was a real suffering—leading them and many others to despair. They both thought that if there were no God then existence was absurd: so they planned to commit suicide unless they were able to find meaning in life. Providentially, it was at this point that they began to study with Henri Bergson (who became a world famous philosopher).

Bergson was a Jew who was eventually drawn to the Catholic faith. He convinced Jacques and Raissa that the human mind can know reality and even reach the absolute. He claimed that "in the absolute we live, and move, and have our being." Raissa said that "we went to Bergson's classes filled with overwhelming curiosity and a sacred expectation. We returned, carrying our little bouquet of truths or of promises, as though vitalized by healthful air – exuberant, prolonging to great and still greater lengths our commentaries upon the

---

[31] From *We Have Been Friends Together: Memoirs Raissa Maritain*, trans. by Julie Kernan (New York: Longmans, Green and Co., 1941).

master's teaching. Winter was passing away; spring was coming."

While attending his lectures, Bergson disproved mechanistic and materialistic theories and proved the freedom of the will. At the same time, he was teaching a course on Plotinus; this great philosopher of the 3rd century A.D. had a passionate and mystical sense of what he called The One – a being in some ways like the God of Christianity. Reading the *Enneads* of Plotinus, Raissa suddenly felt such a wave of joy that she kissed the pages and felt her heart burning with love. After reading Plotinus, Raissa went on to Plato and Pascal, the great scientist and Catholic apologist.

After being engaged for two years, Jacques and Raissa married in 1904. Around the time of Jacques finishing his studies, they met the novelist Léon Bloy who would come to be the most influential person in their spiritual journey into the Catholic Church. Before meeting Bloy, they had thought of Catholicism as coming from the darkness of the Middle Ages and the exploitation of the rich and priestly classes of the poor. In Bloy's writings and personality, they discovered burning zeal and love for Christ combined with a horror of human injustice. Through reading the books of Bloy, they came to appreciate the richness of the Bible. A visit to the Cathedral of Chartres gave the Maritains a visual sense of what they were being drawn to.

Raissa had a mystical experience of the presence of God: she saw a forest as pointing to its Creator. Jacques—who would become one of the greatest 20th century Catholic philosophers of the movement called Neo-Thomism—called this experience a 'metaphysical experience.' She recognized that all things do not come into being of themselves but come into being by God. At this time, Jacques begin to pray: "My God, if You exist, and if You are the truth, make me know it."

Under these influences, little by little, "the hierarchy of spiritual, intellectual, scientific values was revealed to us , and we . . . saw clearly that the truth of one could not be the enemy of the truth of the others." Around this time, Léon Bloy began to introduce them to the saints and mystics of the Church. They began to long to believe the teachings underlying such heroes and their experiences. These great mystics were experiencing the God they were seeking through the mind: in them the mind was serving the relationship between Creator and created.

What led them from speculation to baptism was when Raissa became dangerously ill. During this time, Léon Bloy's wife placed a medal of Mary around her neck. Raissa recovered from the illness. Afterwards they decided to be baptized, but they still felt repugnance for the Church in its concrete form. They still thought of the Church as the society of the bourgeois and lacking in the intellectual life so familiar to Jacques the philosopher.

Finally they decided to put baptism to the test; they followed the truths of the Church so they would discover the meaning of the commitment. So in 1906, Raissa, her sister, and Jacques were baptized in Paris. At this moment of baptism, Raissa recounts that "an immense peace descended upon us, bringing with it the treasures of Faith. There were no more questions, no more anguish, no more trials – there was only the infinite answer of God."

Dorothy Day (1897-1980): From Left Wing Radical to Catholic Radical Leader[32]

Dorothy Day was brought up in a nominally Christian home of non-Church-goers. Her father was a sportswriter in California and Chicago. As a child she liked to read the Bible and was attracted to the music and ritual of an Episcopal

---

[32] From *The Long Loneliness* (N.Y.: Harper and Brothers, 1952).

Church where she went alone, and even though she thought of herself as an agnostic, she was baptized and confirmed.

By the time she was studying at a university, she got the idea from a professor that religion was for the weak of times now past. She felt she had to turn away from it as from a drug—for she accepted the Marxist axiom that "religion was the opiate of the people." As a young woman, she worked as a journalist for Marxist papers. She was not strictly a communist but more of an anarchist of the "Wobblies" kind, who were revolutionary unionists. She also participated in pacifist and suffragette activism.

When Dorothy Day moved back to her birth place, New York City, she worked as a journalist and still though of herself as an agnostic. At this time, she had a love affair resulting in an abortion. Later, she started living with a man who taught her a great love of nature. He was a strong atheist, but this love of nature led her to long to thank God for the beauty of nature. She wondered, "How can there be no God, when there are all these beautiful things?"

Even though so much in love, she felt lonely without a child, and her common-law husband didn't want children because he thought that such an evil world as ours was a terrible place to bring a child into (also, he didn't want the responsibility of raising a child). When she became pregnant, she longed to have this child baptized. Since her common-law husband hated religion, Dorothy was afraid of losing him if she, herself, became a Catholic. But while studying the faith as preparation for having her daughter baptized, she was moved to Catholic theism.

Because of the closeness of people in the socialist movements she was part of, she wanted to be part of the community of the Church and not a loner, and she wanted to share her love of God with others. Dorothy Day became a Catholic in 1927.

Still a radical, even though a Catholic by conviction, Day became a leader of the Catholic Worker Movement— with the help of Peter Maurin, a French radical. She championed resistance to the draft and other social justice causes; she started a hospitality house and soup kitchen for the poor of NYC. And her spirituality was grounded in the traditions of the Church. She became a Benedictine Oblate, went to daily Mass, loved the rosary, and often went to confession.

C.S. Lewis (1898-1963): From Philosophical Atheist to Christian Apologist and Best-Selling Fiction Writer[33]

C.S. Lewis was born in Belfast and baptized into the Church of Ireland. His parents were not very religious, though his mother was the daughter of a Church of Ireland minister. After his mother's death in 1908, Lewis felt estranged from God as he had begged God to heal her. Later he came to believe that all religions were mythical illusions and that the world was too evil for there to be a God.

Having been homeschooled while his mother was alive, Lewis hated the schools he attended until he went to a private tutor, William Kirkpatrick, who taught him how to debate logically and to analyze and refute things. Kirkpatrick was also a thorough atheist and skeptic. At this point, even though Lewis was in total disbelief, he allowed himself to be confirmed and receive Holy Communion to please his father.

As an atheist, Lewis enjoyed the freedom from the fear of God, but his love of poetry and literature helped to keep him from being too materialistic, and as a result of reading George MacDonald's *Phantastes* at sixteen years old, he discovered that he could love goodness for its own sake (he said that MacDonald had baptized his imagination). During his time of

---

[33] From *Surprised by Joy: The Shape of my Early Life* (N.Y.: Book of the Month Club, 1955).

military service in WWI, he came upon a man who was as scholarly and intelligent as himself but who also loved moral virtue. This stunned Lewis who had by no means pursued virtues such as chastity and duty the way his new theistic friend did. Upon his return to Oxford after the war, he continue to develop friendships with people who valued virtue. And Lewis was shocked to find that some of his best friends were actually Christians. Many of his favorite writers were also Christians—such as Milton, MacDonald, Chesterton, Donne, and George Herbert. Gradually he came to see that it was God who was the source of the joy he had been seeking his entire life—especially since peace and happiness had been taken from him with his mother's death.

Lewis is famous for his initial reaction to his conversion to theism (though not yet to the God of Christianity) when he wrote that he was "the most dejected and reluctant convert in all England." Soon after, various experiences and thoughts converged to bring Lewis to see that it was not enough to contemplate an Absolute Being, but one must follow this Being in some way. He came to see that God is "the Lord" and that this Lord wanted to be part of his life—and not only. Indeed, Lewis found that this God wanted to take over his entire life. Lewis was finally graced with belief in Christ and in the Church for reasons best found by reading one of his masterpieces, *Mere Christianity*.

Anthony Flew (1923-2010): From Philosophical Atheism to Theism

The problem of raising believing children is a real one, and this seems especially true of people like David, Saul, Eli, and the many children of ministers. The famous atheist Anthony Flew was the son of minister and theologian. He was born in London and declared himself an atheist while in his middle teen years. Flew was an officer in the Royal Air Force during World War II, and afterward he enrolled in Oxford. As an undergraduate, he attended the Socratic Club meetings lead by C. S. Lewis, and while he had a great deal of respect for Lewis, he disagreed with him about the existence of God.

As a graduate student, Flew studied under the famous philosopher Gilbert Ryle. Later he became a profess of philosophy at Christ Church, Oxford and at other universities. In *God and Philosophy* and *The Presumption of Atheism,* Flew argued that one should presuppose atheism until evidence of a God surfaces, and he was critical of the idea of life after death and the free will defense to the problem of evil. Only the scientific forms of the teleological argument ultimately impressed Flew as decisive.

Shortly have a debate with Gary Habermass in 2003, Flew called his friend to tell him that he was considering becoming a theist. While Flew did not change his position at that time, he concluded that certain philosophical and scientific considerations were causing him to do some serious rethinking. He characterized his position as that of atheism standing in tension with several huge question marks.

At the end of 2004, "Atheist Becomes Theist – Exclusive Interview with Former Atheist Antony Flew" was published in *Philosophia Christi.* Flew agreed to this title. In the article Flew states that he has left his long-standing espousal of atheism by endorsing a deism of the sort that Thomas Jefferson advocated. In a different article, Flew stated that "I think that the most impressive arguments for God's existence are those that are supported by recent scientific discoveries . . . [and] I think the argument to Intelligent Design is enormously stronger than it was when I first met it."[34] Flew's change of mine began with one piece of evidence that troubled him: "the apparent impossibility of providing a naturalistic theory of the origin from DNA of the first

---

[34] http://www.bpnews.net/printerfriendly.asp?id=19712

reproducing species . . . [was] the only reason which I have for beginning to think of believing in a First Cause god is the impossibility of providing a naturalistic account of the origin of the first reproducing organisms."[35] God was the answer to his question of how can something come from nothing.

John C.H. Wu (1899-1937): From Eastern Spirituality to the Catholic Church[36]

Whether one should consider John Wu as turning from atheism to theism or more from Eastern spiritualties to Theism depends a lot on ones view of the nature of Confucian, Taoist and Buddhist thought. As explained in Chapter 1 of Wu's autobiography, there is much controversy about this. Born in China, Wu's life is fascinating: he was a legal and literary genius, and he journeyed from traditional Chinese ritual practices to various ethical philosophies to Methodist Christianity and eventually to the Catholic Church. He began in pantheism with a hedonistic life style and found his home in the fully theistic Catholic faith. He considered the Catholic religion to transcend Eastern and Western cultures including everything good in each.

John Wu was born in Ningpo, China to a traditional family. His father was a poor man who became a banker and benefactor of the poor. As was the custom, Wu was engaged to his future wife at 6 years old. They never met until their wedding day. (Although their marriage was rocky—especially during the time Wu became a rich judge with intimate relationships with other women—their love was renewed and flourished beautifully after his full conversion.) In 1917, John Wu enrolled in a law school in Shanghai under the auspices of

---

[35]
https://www.apologeticspress.org/apcontent.aspx?category=12&article=1467

[36] From *Beyond East and West* (N.Y. Sheed and Ward: 1951).

the American Methodist Mission. It was there that he "fell in love with" reading the Bible (any years later he translated the New Testament into Chinese). He learned about the Trinity and about Christ and was baptized in 1917.

However, when he studied in the United States, he gradually lost this Christian faith and adopted, in its place, a kind of poetical pantheism—each of us a little god, part of a general divine energy. But he was restless, and though he searched for God-substitutes they left him empty. He didn't find that delight in the cosmos was enough. When he returned to China, he became a rich lawyer. In spite of being married with children (13 in all), he lived a dissolute life:

> I had become a regular playboy. For two and a half years I was out practically every night. Even to think of those days smells hell. All the time I was utterly unhappy and dissatisfied with myself, but I was not able to pull my feet out of the mud. The more unhappy I was the more eagerly I sought after pleasures...It was a terrible whirlpool that I was in. I became a prey to the sense of despair. Whenever anybody talked religion to me, I would get into a temper..."He got involved with horoscopes and telling fortunes. He regretted having married an uneducated woman. He thought of divorce but his conscience forbade it. He neglected his wife, children and other family members. He grieved when he read in his daughter's diary that she thought her family was miserable with a father never at home and mother always weeping. After his conversion John would write, "With Christ, the home is a prelude to Heaven. Without Christ, it is prelude to Hell." (133-137).

But he had had enough of Hell on earth.

In Wu's book about his conversion he includes a short explanation of the religions of China. With grace, Catholic mystical saints came into the union with the divine for which Buddha so yearned. From Buddhism, Wu inherited "an intense longing for the 'Other Shore,' which is but another name and a faint foreshadowing of the Kingdom of God which is within us" (p. 185).

By the year 1935 as well as being a minister of education, Wu became part of a group that started a literary, spiritual and culture journal. In spite of all the joy this gave him, he kept restlessly searching for God, until he realized that God was pursuing him, as in the famous poem of Francis Thompson: The Hound of Heaven.

Wu's return—a returning of the prodigal son—was quickened by certain readings: Newman, Papini (*the Life of Christ*), and William James. From Newman's writings, Wu began to understand better why it was necessary to have a source of infallible teachings. From reading Papini's moving account of the conversion of Mary Magdalene, Wu was flooded with repentance. Reading about the sinful Magdalene,

I burst into a violent fit of weeping myself. I said, 'Jesus, I, too, am a prostitute. God has endowed me with beauties of soul and intellect, and I have wasted them on the search for worldly honors and material riches. In the world of politics and in social life, I too have been forced to pretend a pleasure I did not feel, and to show a smiling face to those whom I despised. And all the time I have been neglecting you, my Redeemer and my Spouse. Forgive me, Jesus, and let me anoint you with my tears . . .. When I had uttered this prayer, my soul was inundated with such joy and consolation that tears of gratitude gushed from the bottom of my heart to join the tears of repentance. I felt at that moment that Christ had received me again with His open arms. I experienced such an ecstasy of joy that I can never forget it (235-236).

From reading William James' *Varieties of Religious Experience*, he came to see that with his melancholic soul, that no kind of optimism could ever rescue him. The famous classic of James includes many accounts of the mystical joys of Catholic saints. It also led him to studying the Catholic poet, Dante. Just at this time he visited a deeply Catholic family who introduced him to St. Therese of Lisieux. This saint's total confidence in the mercy of God gave him the courage to seek to become a Catholic, and later, due to a miraculous healing of a dying baby after prayers to St. Therese, the whole family came into the Church. As a return gift for the graces of conversion, Wu made a definitive translation into beautiful Chinese of the Psalms and the New Testament.

The dramatic life of John Wu continued with he and his family's flight from the Japanese during the Sino-Japanese War and, later, moving the whole family to Rome as he became the Chinese Ambassador to the Vatican. He wrote,

With Christ, there is peace even in war. Without Christ, there is war even in peace. With Christ, the poor are rich. Without Christ, the rich are poor. With Christ, adversity is sweet. Without Christ, prosperity is bitter. With Christ, the ignorant are wise. Without Christ, the wise are fools. With Christ, life is a prelude to Heaven. Without Christ, life is a prelude to Hell. (p. 307)

Aleksandr I. Solzhenitsyn (1918-2008): From Communist to Christian Protester

Solzhenitsyn was one of the most famous anti-Communist Russians of the twentieth century. He was brought up in a strong Orthodox religious family, but became an atheist Marxist during his university years. He was a high school teacher before World War II, and during World War II, he became a soldier until his arrest in 1945 for criticizing the communist regime. Although there was not enough evidence to convict him, he nevertheless had to serve eight years in prison doing extremely hard manual labor until he was transferred to the research institute that he would later described in his famous novel *The First Circle*.

During his prison years, he was drawn back to belief in God. Solzhenitsyn also started writing in secret, hiding pages he would use later by keeping them in miniature print rolled up into the cuffs of his trousers. After his release, he tried to publish in the Soviet Union, but his books were suppressed. Eventually, he was able to smuggle some of his book out to the West. There was enormous excitement in the United States and Europe because he proved that all the evils we thought were true about atheistic communism were even worse than we imagined.

Solzhenitsyn won the Nobel Prize in 1970 and was exiled to Germany in 1974. He eventually settled in the United States with his family in 1976 where he lived in semi-seclusion in Vermont while working on the history of the Gulag, the network of prison camps covering vast territories of the Soviet Union.

There was some shock when, during a commencement address at Harvard in 1978, Solzhenitsyn said that in spite of the horrors of Communist rule he could not wish his people to have lived those decades, instead, in the decadent West with its vapid life-style of consumerism. On the other hand, there was great joy among Christians to see that this famous humanistic protestor against atheistic communism had become a theist. And he put his new faith and hope into words: "No one on earth has any other way left but upward to God. Reach up and take the warm hand of God."

In 1990 he was admitted back to the Soviet Union where he continued writing and also using television as a medium for his continued critique of the ills of society.

Bernard N. Nathanson, M.D. (1926-2011): From Abortionist and Pro-Choice Activist to Pro-Life Activist and Roman Catholic[37]

In the beginning of the *Hand of God*, Bernard Nathanson tells the state of things 40 years into his life: "In 1968, I was one of the three founders of the National Abortion Rights Action League. I ran the largest abortion clinic in the United States, and as its director I oversaw tens of thousands of abortions. I have performed thousands myself. How could this have happened? How could I have done this?" (p. 5)

In his biography he tells about the character of his Jewish family including the suicide of his grandfather and his sister, his only sibling. His father was raised in Canada in an orthodox Jewish family and became a doctor. As a child Nathanson learned much about Judaism since his father insisted that he study it, but the same father also derided orthodoxy—and there was no love of God in the family life or in the services he attended. His father claimed not to believe in God but in some superior power.

Helping to explain his later choices in life, Bernard gives an account of a terrible childhood due to the hatred between his father and mother and the way his father made the two children allies in that hatred. His father also told him that he had extra-marital affairs.

Bernard went to an upper class prep school in NYC and then to Cornell University as a pre-med student. He went to his father's medical school at McGill in Canada. In the process

---

[37] From *The Hand of God* (Washington, D.C.: Regnery Publishing, Inc., 1996).

of his secular education, he lost faith in orthodox Jewish practices even though he still practiced some. He specialized in obstetrics and gynecology in New York City. At medical school Bernard fell in love with Ruth. When she got pregnant, out of wedlock, long before he would be graduating he arranged for an abortion. They both considered it to be a baby and cried over it before and after. Here is how he describes his memory of this occasion:

> Despite her brave face, her loyalty and love . . . I am sure that in some melancholy corridor of her mind lurked the questions: Why didn't he marry me? Why couldn't we have had this baby? Why should I have had to imperil my life and my future children for the sake of his convenience and academic schedule? Will God punish me for what I have done by making me barren? (p. 57)

Since he was an atheist by now, the last question did not concern him. But the suffering that he causes did not end there: "This served as my introductory excursion into the satanic world of abortion. Nor was that the end of it for me personally . . . after 2 ruined marriages destroyed largely by my own selfish narcissism and inability to love." He impregnated another a woman who loved him very much and begged to keep the baby, but since he was just building his career, he told her he would not marry her and couldn't afford to support a child: "an egregious example of the coercion exercised by males in the abortion tragedy." (p. 58-61). And he performed the abortion himself.

Nathanson describes the gruesome technique of the abortion and how coolly this was accomplished without the slightest regrets. He thought of it as doing a service to others. Nathanson's first wife was a Jew of a similar background. He was tired of love affairs and of living in the cramped quarters of an intern at a hospital. They seemed to get along well, though he did not really love her. He married her with the idea that if it didn't work he could divorce her. They agreed not to have a child. They divorced after 4 ½ years.

He would marry a non-Jew next. His father totally rejected him for marrying a woman who was not Jewish. He even black-balled him in their common medical profession. At Woman's Hospital in Harlem where he was practicing he came to know more of the plight of the poor. Many of these were victims of botched illegal abortions. The horrible condition of these women was the main factor in leading Nathanson to champion legal abortion by expanding the already existing legal abortions done for the incest, rape, and fetal deformity, and threat to the life and health of the mother.

In 1967, he met Lawrence Lader, an admirer of Margaret Sanger and founder of Planned Parenthood. Lader had written a book on how laws prohibiting abortion could be changed. Out of the long collaboration between Nathanson and Lader came NARAL, the National Association for Repeal of Abortion Laws. Their goal was abortion on demand. This group was virulently anti-Catholic—blaming the deaths of women in botched abortions on the Church because it prohibited abortion. NARAL contributed to the passage of the legalization of abortion in the Supreme Court Decision of Roe v. Wade.

Nathanson would perform thousands of abortions and administer facilities that performed tens of thousands of them. In 1972, due to ultra-sound making it possible to view babies in the womb, Nathanson began to bond with these tiny humans. In 1974, he wrote an article for a medical journal questioning the morality of abortion. "There is no longer serious doubt in my mind that human life exists within the womb from the very onset of pregnancy" (p. 126). This article unleashed storms of rage from doctors who had originally despised Nathanson as the abortion king, but had since accepted it and wanted to continue receiving the money that came from it. Nathanson received death threats. Still justifying abortion in special circumstances, in 1979 he performed his last abortion because he insisted that abortion was waging war against defenseless human. The film *The Silent Scream* was made by Nathanson to show the world what abortion really is.

How did all this lead Nathanson to become a theist and then a Roman Catholic? For years of not doing abortions, Nathanson experienced terrible guilt and despair. He contemplated suicide. But instead he decided that doing pro-life work made it important to continue to live. He also felt terrible about his divorces: two subsequent marriages had failed mostly due to his faults. He became impressed with the goodness of religious pro-lifers, especially the joy they had in prayer when doing Operation Rescues:

> For the first time in my entire adult life, I began to entertain seriously the notion of God – a god who problematically had led me through the proverbial circles of hell, only to show me the way to redemption and mercy through His grace. The thought violated every 18th century certainty I had cherished; it instantly converted my past into a vile bog of sin and evil; it indicted me and convicted me of high crimes against those who had loved me, and against those whom I did not even know; and simultaneously – miraculously – it held out a shimmering sliver of Hope to me, in the growing belief that Someone had died for my sins and my evil two millennia ago. (p. 193-194)

He then started reading the stories of converts to theism, and he became a Catholic in 1996.

I, Dr. Ronda, met Nathanson before his conversion at a conference. Knowing he would speak, I brought him a book I had edited of conversions of Jews to the Catholic Faith. He

smiled when I offered it to him. "I read it already, Ronda." He
asked a Jewish convert friend of mine why she had become a
Catholic instead of a Protestant. He liked her answer,
"Catholicism is Christianity with a mind." But Nathanson,
after his conversion, claimed that his real reason for
becoming a Catholic was that no other religion offers as much
forgiveness.

Eldridge Cleaver (1935-1998): From Black Panther and Communist to Christian Prison Minister[38]

Eldridge Cleaver was raised in Los Angeles. His mother was a strong Christian, but his father was a physically abusive man who used to hit his mother. This parent also regularly beat Eldridge for defiance. When his father beat his mother, the boy would hit him back. Finally, when Eldridge was a strong enough, he decided to beat his father to death. But the day he decided to kill his father the next time he hit him, his father didn't beat him but, instead, left home for 5 years.

Eldridge then began to direct his violence elsewhere with rape, drug-dealing, and other crimes. Eventually he was sent to prison. (Writing about his life after his conversion, Cleaver insists that only Jesus Christ can redirect the personality of a criminal mind.) In prison Cleaver resolved to become a revolutionary to defeat the ruling class. During this time, Cleaver married a black-activist, Kathleen Cleaver, and he financed his revolutionary groups by income from his best-selling book *Soul on Ice*. In this book Cleaver described the appeal of the Black Moslem movement. Elijah Mohammed bonded blacks together and insisted that drugs, shooting, and drinking brawls had to stop. He claimed that it was the white devils who were trying to burn out the blacks through drugs and crime. The blacks were losers this way. Cleaver did not

---

[38] From *Soul on Fire* (Waco, Texas: Word Books, 1978).

start the Panthers but joined them, impressed by their courage in carrying guns openly.

In various stays in prison, Cleaver started reading books, especially Marxist ones. Positively, the Panthers wanted freedom, release of all prisoners unjustly tried, black juries, and land.

Eventually out of prison, but sought by the police, Cleaver decided to break his bond and flee from the US to Cuba. Cleaver lauded Communist heroes such as Stalin and Mao. He travelled for the Panthers from Cuba to Algeria and from Korea, to China, to North Vietnam. Eventually he would see that the corruption of the communists was as violent and inhumane as the powers they replaced. For example, he found that the guerillas in Cuba were racists. Castro shipped blacks off to Africa. In the Asian communist countries, he could see that they had no tradition of individual rights. In America you could protest the betrayal of the American dream as it affected blacks, but in Communist countries there was no such ideal to appeal to. A fascinating side-effect of the trial of the Nixon aides was that blacks could see that the most powerful man in the country could be brought down by justice. The Constitution proved stronger than Nixon. Eventually, after living in Communist countries he would say, "I would rather be in prison in America than free somewhere else" (p. 98).

One of the greatest factors leading to Cleaver's rethinking about life was the birth of his son and daughter who seemed like miracles. Because of his children, Cleaver began to think there was a designer God. The children had souls. This truth was contrary to his previous anti-religious ideas.

In 1972 he was living with his family under a false name in Paris. He couldn't return to the States without serving his prison sentence. He started to become empty and restless. He was impressed that Nixon was out and the FBI was being reformed. His old revolutionary friends were becoming leaders of cities. He became depressed and thought of suicide. One

96 | C a t h o l i c   R e a l i s m :   a   F r a m e w o r k   f o r   t h e
R e f u t a t i o n   o f   A t h e i s m   a n d   t h e   E v a n g e l i z a t i o n
o f   A t h e i s t s

night in France, Cleaver went outside to look at the sky, and he was staring

> at the moon from a balcony and he saw his face in it and then his fallen heroes, Castro, Mao, Marx . . . passing in review—each one appearing for a moment of time, and then dropping out of sight, like fallen heroes. Finally at the end of the procession, in dazzling, shimmering light, the image of Jesus Christ appeared. That was the last straw. I just crumbled and started crying. I fell to my knee . . . and in the midst of this shaking and crying, the Lord's Prayer and the 23rd Psalm came into my mind. I hadn't thought about these prayers for years. I started repeating them, and after a time I . . . jumped up and ran to my bookshelf and got the Bible. It was the family Bible my mother had given to me . . . That night I slept the most peaceful sleep I have ever known in my life . . . in the morning I could see in my mind the way, all the way back home . . . I saw a path of light that ran through a prison cell . . . This prison cell was a dark spot on this path of light, and the meaning, which was absolutely clear to me, was that I didn't have to wait on any politician to help me get back home. I had it within my power to get back home by taking that first step, by surrendering; it was a certainty that everything was going to be all right." (p. 212)

But people thought he had sold out; however, he replied that he had sold out to Jesus.

Arrested on landing in NYC, he still "felt free because of God" (p.220). Some Panthers denounced him as a FBI informer. His old friends wouldn't visit him. Because of this he turned more and more to God. Alone in his cell he asked Jesus to be his personal savior and take away his sins. He cried with tears of joy. Soon he was making new friends in Christ. After nine months of prison, he was out on bail on the generosity of a Christian friend. He got to see his mother who had prayed for her prodigal son for 30 years.

He was so strong in the Lord that he could enjoy having a prayer session arranged by Colson, the ex-convict Nixon aide, with a former Ku Klux Klan leader. All three now born again—Jesus healed their wounds, forgave their sins, and brought them together. Cleaver then entered into a crusade against violence. This man who had spent almost half his life in prison wrote: "The Lord has transported me from world revolutions to a radical dependence on his transforming power" (p. 237).

Elizabeth Fox-Genovese (1941-2007): From Cultural Non-believing Christian to Catholic[39]

Elizabeth Fox-Genovese was the Eléonore Raoul Professor of the Humanities at Emory University, where she was the founding director of the Institute for Women's Studies. She also served as editor of *The Journal of The Historical Society*. Elizabeth Fox-Genovese was the author of *Women and the Future of the Family* (2000), *"Feminism is Not the Story of My Life": How the Feminist Elite Has Lost Touch With the Real Concerns of Women* (1996), *Feminism Without Illusions: A Critique of Individualism* (1991), and *Within the Plantation Household: Black and White Women of the Old South* (1988), which received the C. Hugh Holman Prize of the Society for the Society of Southern Literature, the Julia Cherry Spruill Prize of the Southern Association of Women Historians, and was named an outstanding book of the year by the Augustus Meyer Foundation for the Study of Human Rights. She also served on the Advisory Board of the Catholic Education Resource Center.

---

[39] The information in this summary is taken from: Elizabeth Fox-Genovese. "A Conversion Story" *First Things* 102 (April 2000): 39-43.

Born in Boston in May 28, 1941, Elizabeth Fox-Genovese was known as a prolific writer whose major themes included women's issues and feminism. She grew up in a non-Christian, non-believing home, acknowledging that her self-identity as a Christian was only culturally based; nevertheless, she was familiar with foundational aspects of Christianity. The realization that societal norms around her generated the simultaneous upholding of various viewpoints caused her to question the validity of the ideological basis behind this stance.

Her intellectual probing led her understand there was something innately wrong in the relativistic mentality that surrounded her. In the midst of her feministic writing pursuits, she began to appreciate the value of unborn life while investigating different angles of women's issues. These topics and others, including the right to assisted suicide, allowed her to understand the existence of the utilitarian agenda hidden in the semantics that promoted these "rights".

The culmination of her intellectual search occurred in 1995 when she decided attend a Mass at the Cathedral of Christ the King in Atlanta, together with her un-believing spouse and a Catholic friend. She relates that one of the factors that led her to a deeper faith was prompted by recognizing the intellectual conceit enveloping the academic environment in secular institutions: "An important part of what opened me to Catholicism—and to the peerless gift of faith in Christ Jesus—was my growing horror at the pride of too many in the secular academy. The sin is all the more pernicious because it is so rarely experienced as sin." Her words disclose a keen awareness of the experiential dimension that frequently disguises evil as good—language covers up a real problem.

In the same way, her exposure to "radical, upscale feminism" provided a deeper recognition of the arrogant attitude at the root of such ideologies. She contrasted feminist predispositions with the Gospel message's premise regarding the Savior's mission to serve. Additionally, her study of Saint John Paul II's writings familiarized her with his focus of self-gift as it relates to the concept of the person. Furthermore, her meditation of the first beatitude made her understand that "the determination of worth" belongs to God, not to the person.

Elizabeth Fox-Genovese died in Atlanta on January 2, 2007. Her writings certainly angered many radical feminists and attracted "conservative" ones. An extract of her obituary summarizes her quest for truth: "Reason led her to the door of faith, and prayer enabled her to walk through it. As she herself described her conversion from secularism to Catholicism, it had a large intellectual component; yet it was, in the end, less her choice than God's grace."[40]

Rev. Charles Goraieb (1947-Present): From New Age Hippie to Catholic Priest[41]

Fr. Goraieb's story begins with a familiar struggle of youth—to find meaning for his life. He came of age in the late 1960's, when protesting the Vietnam War and participating in the cultural revolution were the rites of passage for his generation. Growing up in Southern California in the 60's and 70's, where every new and bizarre idea found a ready audience, added yet another dimension.

To keep his growing anxiety manageable, Goraieb had become increasingly dependent on marijuana, which only made things worse. As college graduation approached, he had to decide what my next step would be. One ray of hope came

---

[40] Robert P. George, The Story of a Well-Lived Life Elizabeth Fox-Genovese, R.I.P at National Review, January 3, 2007 at http://www.nationalreview.com/articles/219635/story-well-lived-life/robert-p-george#.

[41] Taken from My Story, *by Fr. Charlie Goraieb, Pastor St. Timothy's Church in Mesa, Arizona Parish Bulletin, 2012.*

from reading Henry David Thoreau's *Walden*, which painted the portrait of a serene, idyllic life of peaceful solitude. He left LA for the mellow, college town of Santa Cruz, located on the coast about 100 miles South of San Francisco, where he hoped to find his *Walden*.

There are some things that can only be learned by life experiences. For instance, beautiful surroundings don't necessarily translate to inner peace. He did manage to find his way into a commune populated by other cultural runaways and lived among them in a tee-pee. From afar, it seemed as if I had found the Rosetta stone—living amidst the majestic redwood trees and abiding by the dictates of *The Whole Earth Catalogue*, the hippie's bible. He had become a vegetarian, learned to sing to the moon inebriated on cheap wine, and fashioned himself to be an *avant garde*, cultural front-runner. But he had sunk deeper into the drug culture, got his heart broken and returned the favor to a few others. And he was still miserable. Among the Spiritual groups he tried, some were guided by Zen or the I-Ching or the Bible along with doses of Yoga or Transcendental Meditation. All were very stimulating and interesting, but his search was not over.

During one of his conversations with a Christian leader of one of these communes, he looked intently at him and challenged him to read the New Testament. He said that if he were to do so, he guaranteed that Goraieb would find the peace he had been looking for. Something about his challenge convinced Goraieb that to give it a try.

In the New Testament letter to the Hebrews, it says that the word of God *cuts sharper than a two edged sword*. Goraieb was about to discover how true those words are. Provided with a pocket-sized, King James version of the New Testament, he began reading the Gospel of Matthew. It didn't take long to get drawn into the narrative. For some time now Goraieb had been reading the books of the acclaimed gurus and had listened attentively to numerous sages and would-be prophets. This time, with the Gospel of Matthew, something different was about to happen.

There were three related but distinct events that built on each other. First was his fascination with the astounding wisdom and the beauty of all that Jesus said. The Sermon on the Mount simply stunned me. I recalled having heard it before in church (I came from a Catholic family) but now, for the first time, I was reading this astounding discourse in context.

Jesus' wisdom was amazing and irresistibly inspiring. But it wasn't just the ideas or the account of Jesus' miracles that captured Goraieb—it was Jesus *Himself*. What emerged from the Gospel was an extraordinarily attractive figure whose manner and qualities were unlike anyone he had ever encountered, and sometime after reading the New Testament—without warning or preparation and while traveling—Jesus, the Son of God, *spoke* to him.

Goraieb actually heard the voice of God addressed to him. There were others in the room when it happened, but no one else heard him. It would have been easy to dismiss it as a chemically-induced illusion except that about a month before he had decided to purify his body and completely abstain from all drugs and alcohol.

The voice was not audible, but words were spoken to him by another. The actual words were quite simple: *I love you and am your Lord.* No great revelation here, but he point is that Jesus, the Son of God, had spoken those words to *him*, Charlie Goraieb, a self-willed, sinful and rebellious cast-about.

For reasons that he may never understand, God chose him as one to whom He would reveal his Divine Presence....The effect of his encounter with the Lord was to lift the cloud of doubt, anger, confusion and fear that had settled over him the last few years. Instead, he was now filled with joy and purpose. Shortly after this, Goraieb was befriended by a Catholic priest. Charlie had been baptized Catholic but left during college. This priest helped him come back to the Church. The Holy Spirit led him into a Charismatic Catholic community. For 11 years he lived as a single for the Lord with other charismatic men, and he said,

> Often times people we prayed with would talk about how much they had suffered and how they wanted to put that behind them and connect with God. Of course what they needed was to make a good confession that would lift so much of their burden, but it was not easy trying to explain this, much less getting them to see a priest. How wonderful, I thought to myself, if I could be the one to give them the gift of absolution...Was it possible that God was calling me, with all that I had lived through, to become a Catholic priest?
>
> This would no doubt be the most radical and unlikely choice of my life. But as I tested the idea in the light of my relationship with Jesus Christ, it made perfect sense. Well, maybe "sense" is not the right word, because up to that point, my life had not followed a sensible trajectory. But it was the Lord who was putting the pieces together and casting a vision for me to follow. If I was willing to step out of the boat and walk towards his outstretched hand, it was possible that I would be able to share in his priesthood and ministry.
>
> I was already living a life of celibacy, so that would not be a problem. In return, I would be able to speak for Him, make him present in the sacraments and absolve sins. Yes, this was starting to make a lot of sense.

His calculations went something like this: if he had heard him wrong and the priesthood was not for me that would become clear both to him and others at the seminary. The risk of loss was very low. But if he had gotten it right, it would mean unimaginable joy and the privilege of being consecrated for his service. He liked his chances.

And so began his next big journey, to the seminary to begin his studies for the priesthood. He often wondered what his old friends would have said about this new phase. One of them who did make it to his ordination said that he went to extremes like no one he had ever known. "I smiled, knowing that what I really had done was take small, sequential steps led by the Master Guide."

I knew Charlie when he was a single man in the charismatic community. He became an incredibly zealous, loving, Catholic priest in the Diocese of Phoenix, Arizona.

Chapter 3: Catholic Realism: Proof and Attributes

"The worst moment for the atheist is when he is really thankful and has nobody to thank." -- Dante Gabriel Rossetti (1828-1882), qtd. by G. K. Chesterton in *St. Francis of Assisi* (1923)

"If there were no God, there would be no Atheists." -- G. K. Chesterton (1874-1936), *Where All Roads Lead*, London (1922)

"We are all atheists about most of the gods that societies have ever believed in. Some of us just go one god further." -- Richard Dawkins (1941 -), "The Root of All Evil", UK Channel 4, (2006)

God's Identity

The God of Love described in Scripture corresponds to the God who must be good for one fundamental reason: evil is a privation, and an absolute being cannot be lacking in love, omnipotence, or omniscience. Do we not always think that if someone is being extremely unloving then a good heart is lacking? If someone is even just a little unloving, then a privation exists. God is the absolute being, a conscious personal Creator of the Universe. If God is just a force then God is *less* than a human. If you say God might exist but not the theistic God of the Abrahamic tradition, then you are really saying a God may exist that you do not have to obey since you owe no existence to him. From God being a necessary, or absolute, being, it follows that God cannot be lacking in anything since all things must proceed from God.

True theists understand that an absolute being exists who created us for the purpose of entering into a loving relationship with Him, but the various privations of theism—which we call various kinds of atheism—detract from an authentic understanding of who God is, which necessarily also detracts from an authentic understanding of who we are because we are necessarily dependent beings. We are not our own creators.

The more heretical a person's beliefs about God, the more he or she would seem to be right in rejecting any belief in a God that is nothing more than a mental construct. Concerning the idea of God that most atheists seem to be rejecting, we can honestly say that we, too, are atheists in that we do not belief in false truth. We do not, that is, believe in what they conceive to be the God that they reject.

In the third chapter of *The God Delusion,* Richard Dawkins states that "[t]he five 'proofs' asserted by Thomas Aquinas in the thirteenth century don't prove anything, and are easily – though I hesitate to say so, given his eminence – exposed as vacuous" (p. 100). Dawkins then lumps the first three together as "just different ways of saying the same thing," ridicules the fourth one as "fatuous", and considers the fifth one as having been "blown out of the water" by Darwin. So, what are these five proofs, or "ways," that Dawkins so cleverly "destroys" in only a few pages of text? They are, namely, the following from Question 2, Article 3, of the first part of the Summa Theologica.[42]

---

[42] St. Thomas, *Summa Theologica*, NewAdvent.org, http://newadvent.org/summa/1002.htm.

1. The Unmoved Mover

The first and more manifest way is the argument from motion.
It is certain, and evident to our senses, that in the world some
things are in motion. Now whatever is in motion is put in
motion by another, for nothing can be in motion except it is in
potentiality to that towards which it is in motion; whereas a
thing moves inasmuch as it is in act. For motion is nothing else
than the reduction of something from potentiality to actuality.
But nothing can be reduced from potentiality to actuality,
except by something in a state of actuality. Thus that which is
actually hot, as fire, makes wood, which is potentially hot, to
be actually hot, and thereby moves and changes it. Now it is
not possible that the same thing should be at once in actuality
and potentiality in the same respect, but only in different
respects. For what is actually hot cannot simultaneously be
potentially hot; but it is simultaneously potentially cold. It is
therefore impossible that in the same respect and in the same
way a thing should be both mover and moved, i.e. that it
should move itself. Therefore, whatever is in motion must be
put in motion by another. If that by which it is put in motion
be itself put in motion, then this also must needs be put in
motion by another, and that by another again. But this cannot
go on to infinity, because then there would be no first mover,
and, consequently, no other mover; seeing that subsequent
movers move only inasmuch as they are put in motion by the
first mover; as the staff moves only because it is put in motion
by the hand. Therefore it is necessary to arrive at a first mover,
put in motion by no other; and this everyone understands to
be God.

2. The Uncaused Cause

The second way is from the nature of the efficient cause. In the
world of sense we find there is an order of efficient causes.

107 | Catholic Realism: a Framework for the
Refutation of Atheism and the Evangelization
of Atheists

There is no case known (neither is it, indeed, possible) in which a thing is found to be the efficient cause of itself; for so it would be prior to itself, which is impossible. Now in efficient causes it is not possible to go on to infinity, because in all efficient causes following in order, the first is the cause of the intermediate cause, and the intermediate is the cause of the ultimate cause, whether the intermediate cause be several, or only one. Now to take away the cause is to take away the effect. Therefore, if there be no first cause among efficient causes, there will be no ultimate, nor any intermediate cause. But if in efficient causes it is possible to go on to infinity, there will be no first efficient cause, neither will there be an ultimate effect, nor any intermediate efficient causes; all of which is plainly false. Therefore it is necessary to admit a first efficient cause, to which everyone gives the name of God.

3. The Cosmological Argument

The third way is taken from possibility and necessity, and runs thus. We find in nature things that are possible to be and not to be, since they are found to be generated, and to corrupt, and consequently, they are possible to be and not to be. But it is impossible for these always to exist, for that which is possible not to be at some time is not. Therefore, if everything is possible not to be, then at one time there could have been nothing in existence. Now if this were true, even now there would be nothing in existence, because that which does not exist only begins to exist by something already existing. Therefore, if at one time nothing was in existence, it would have been impossible for anything to have begun to exist; and thus even now nothing would be in existence — which is absurd. Therefore, not all beings are merely possible, but there must exist something the existence of which is necessary. But every necessary thing either has its necessity caused by another, or not. Now it is impossible to go on to infinity in necessary things which have their necessity caused by another, as has been already proved in regard to efficient causes. Therefore we cannot but postulate the existence of some being having of itself its own necessity, and not receiving it from another, but rather causing in others their necessity. This all men speak of as God.

4. The Argument from Degree

The fourth way is taken from the gradation to be found in things. Among beings there are some more and some less good, true, noble and the like. But "more" and "less" are predicated of different things, according as they resemble in their different ways something which is the maximum, as a thing is said to be hotter according as it more nearly resembles that which is hottest; so that there is something which is truest, something best, something noblest and, consequently, something which is uttermost being; for those things that are greatest in truth are greatest in being, as it is written in Metaph. ii. Now the maximum in any genus is the cause of all in that genus; as fire, which is the maximum heat, is the cause of all hot things. Therefore there must also be something which is to all beings the cause of their being, goodness, and every other perfection; and this we call God.

5. The Teleological Argument, or Argument from Design

The fifth way is taken from the governance of the world. We see that things which lack intelligence, such as natural bodies, act for an end, and this is evident from their acting always, or nearly always, in the same way, so as to obtain the best result. Hence it is plain that not fortuitously, but designedly, do they achieve their end. Now whatever lacks intelligence cannot move towards an end, unless it be directed by some being endowed with knowledge and intelligence; as the arrow is shot to its mark by the archer. Therefore some intelligent being exists by whom all natural things are directed to their end; and this being we call God.

All five of these arguments, as Dawkins correctly identifies, are *a posteriori* arguments, or arguments that rely "upon inspection of the world" (p. 104), and that is fitting as that is how we humans learn. Aristotle, a pagan, teaches this from the opening of his *Metaphysics* where he writes, "All men by nature desire to know. An indication of this is the delight we take in our senses; for even apart from their usefulness they are loved for themselves."[43] In short, we come to learn opening our senses to the world, and the perceptions we obtain (for example, our touching a hot stove) bring about an understanding of universal concepts (for example, hotness). We move in this way from the first level of abstraction, which is material existence, the proper study of which is cosmology, to the third level of abstraction, which is immaterial existence, the proper study of which is metaphysics. We can say, then, that through natural reason we come first to know God through his effects, which is through the order, we say, of knowledge. God knows things, though, as their cause, which is through the order, we say, of creation.

Let us go through each of the five.

The First Way concerns the idea of motion and the fact that everything that moves is moved by something else but that eventually, to avoid the impossibility of an infinite regress, we bump up against an unmoved mover. It is that which we call God. When St. Thomas speaks of some things

---

[43] Aristotle, Metaphysics, Book 1, Chapter 1, http://classics.mit.edu/Aristotle/metaphysics.1.i.html

being in motion, he means material things, not, say, self-moving immaterial spiritual entities. When he adds that whatever is in motion was put in motion by something else, the words 'potentiality' and 'act' mean that when something moves from one place to another it has to be potentially where it will end up. For example, a rock is not potentially by itself able to rise into the air, but a balloon on the ground potentially can be flying in the air. The balloon will not rise out of its shrunken original state without the breath of the one who blows it up and the breeze which lifts it. The balloon cannot be simultaneously on the ground and up in the air. It has both 'potentiality' and 'act.' Likewise, a handful of students standing in a line can experience what it is like to be pushed by the student in the front so that each student down the line receives a push. The last student was put in motion by the person pushing all the way back to the first student who pushed. That this cannot go on to infinity backward up the line is self-evident since a first mover is required. Peter Kreeft provides an illustration of this in his *Summa of the Summas* through the example of a train. Without an engine, the cars cannot push one another in an infinite series because there would be no force to start the process into motion. The car with the engine has to be outside the series of box cars.

The Second Way concerns the idea of the nature of the efficient cause; the word "efficient" being one of Aristotle's four causes that also include the formal cause, the material cause and the final cause. To explain the nature of the efficient cause, we can look at the case of a sculptor making a statue, where the hand of the artist and an instrument such as a hammer are the efficient causes. A family tree is also good way to illustrate this idea because one can determine one's lineage as deriving from two people who each derived from another two people and on backwards as far as one's family memory goes. The ancestor whom we cannot remember is in that line, and behind him or her another ancestor that is not known by who existed nonetheless. One does not cause oneself, after all, and the family line did not appear spontaneously at the last memorable ancestor. Since no one can cause himself or herself, or his or her line, to exist out of nothing, we assume that something beyond oneself, or beyond one's line, brought it about, and we cannot take away that cause without also taking away its effect. Ultimate effects, then, point to the existence of intermediate effects, which point to the existence of an original effect brought about by a cause that existed prior to the existence of the original and subsequent effects. An efficient cause by its very definition always has agency, no matter where in the chain of an imaginary-series-called-infinity it lies. It is necessary to understand agency—the ability to "produce change or existence in another" (add footnote for Hardon's dictionary here)—because our very existence depends on it. The power that created the first humans (whom we understand to be Adam and Eve) had agency; therefore, that agent is a powerful, real existent--not just a word like "infinity." Since persons and their family lines exist, they must have been caused; therefore, it is necessary to admit a first efficient cause to which everyone gives the name God. If everything has a cause, though, one might ask whether God also needs a cause, and the basic answer is that only contingent, dependent beings need a cause. In other words, only non-perfect and infinite beings need to be caused.

The Third Way is the argument from contingency, which means simply being dependent vs. independent. For those among our readers who remember the *Twilight Zone* television program, one of the episodes depicted a small town in which one minute all the birds disappeared; in the next moment, all of the grass disappeared; and then all of the houses disappeared. Finally, all that remained was the main character standing at a phone booth getting a canned message. The next screen could obviously be blank. We all know that even the most enduring things like mountains disintegrate slowly; in order words, everything we see could *not have always been*. They are all possible, but none is necessary and eternally enduring. That's contingent being—that which is now but was not before. In an infinite amount of time, each thing at one time would not exist since it does not have absolute necessity of eternal endurance in it. The necessary of existence, or what necessarily must exist in order for all these other things to have come into being, we give the name God. God is that which eternally endures—the only non-contingent being.

The Fourth Way involves gradation, or the distinction of goodness in things. Among beings, there are differences by degree. If we understand that there is something perfect, something that has no blemish, on one end of the spectrum, and something on the other end of the spectrum that is marred beyond recognition, we perceive a range of imperfection. When a silversmith works with silver, for example, he or she notes that the first smelting reveals a number of impurities, more or less depending upon the quality of the original substance. As the impurities are burned off, the molten metal starts to resemble a glassy surface. The silversmith knows the impurities are gone when his or her own image is clearly discernible within the silver. In terms of contingent beings, we know that some have greater goodness in them than do others, and this greater goodness more closely resembles absolute goodness than does lesser goodness. The absolute goodness, which is necessarily the source of all goodness, is what we call God—not just free of imperfection, but radiant

The Fifth Way deals with what St. Thomas calls the governance of the world, or argument by design, for all things act for some end—exhibiting purpose or consistency—such as when planets move according to a pattern or seeds become plants when joined with soil. This natural order in the universe can come about only by design since that which lacks intelligence necessarily needs to be directed to the end that it achieves. A design comes from a designer. We call the designer of the cosmos—of all that is—God.

If you were a traveler in the past who had never seen a watch, for instance, and then came upon one, you might ask someone to explain to you what it was—never thinking that the watch had come about by chance. You would think it had an intelligent creator. By analogy the universe, so intricate in its design, could not have come about by chance, but must have come to be by the work of an Intelligent Mind. "Chance," which is Dawkin's God, is not an entity full of power to create, but merely a word to describe purposeful things coming to exist without any purpose behind them.

Dawkins' idea that the first three of these ways are redundant lacks insight into the very particular nature of each Way and the manner in which all five are intertwined. For example, because of the third way—that all contingent beings are unnecessary—chance and evolution explain nothing because out of nothing comes nothing, not evolving beings.

Is it possible, though, to leap immediately from the philosophical proofs of God's existence to the God of Scripture? Some may do this, but that may be to equate two things one has in mind – the philosophical explanation of the necessity for God and the Scriptural revelation that there is a God. Islamic philosophy, after all, drawn as it was from Aristotle and Plotinus, also demonstrates the Truth and Oneness of God, and the Arabic philosophers of the Golden Age of Islam also held philosophy in one hand and the Qur'an in the other and made an equation that reads very similarly to that of the Christian: "human reason demonstrates the existence of God, and Sacred Scripture as found in this Qur'an is the word of God, so the two go hand in hand – there is nothing in the Qur'an that cannot also be figured out by man, but the Qur'an does it more expeditiously while human reason is a laborious process of demonstration in comparison."

So how is Christianity distinct? One of the things that makes the Christian scriptures different is the allowance of mystery – there are some things, like the existence of the Holy Trinity, the Christian simply would never have figured out without their having been revealed, and even then, the full nature of such things may remain in mystery. To avoid leaping from God conceived through the philosophical process of demonstration to God revealed in Christian scripture, St. Thomas provides a bridge between reason and faith. Namely, he identifies the reason for diversity among created things, following his demonstration of the unity of God who yet has attributes. Diversity is a manifestation of the perfection of God made visible, and diversity in persons allows for interdependence in community. The world is like God, and the likeness is drawn out even more in community (note the *unity* in *community*).

St. Thomas writes of God's unity,

First from His simplicity. For it is manifest that the reason why any singular thing is "this particular thing" is because it cannot be communicated to many: since that whereby Socrates is a man, can be communicated to many; whereas, what makes him this particular man, is only communicable to one. Therefore, if Socrates were a man by what makes him to be this particular man, as there cannot be many Socrates, so there could not in that way be many men. Now this belongs to God alone; for God Himself is His own nature, as was shown above (Question 3, Article 3). Therefore, in the very same way God is God, and He is this God. Impossible is it therefore that many Gods should exist.

Secondly, this is proved from the infinity of His perfection. For it was shown above (Question 4, Article 2) that God comprehends in Himself the whole perfection of being. If then many gods existed, they would necessarily differ from each other. Something therefore would belong to one which did not belong to another. And if this were a privation, one of them would not be absolutely perfect; but if a perfection, one of them would be without it. So it is impossible for many gods to exist. Hence also the ancient philosophers, constrained as it were by truth, when they asserted an infinite principle, asserted likewise that there was only one such principle.

Thirdly, this is shown from the unity of the world. For all things that exist are seen to be ordered to each other since some serve others. But things that are diverse do not harmonize in the same order, unless they are ordered thereto by one. For many are reduced into one order by one better than by many: because one is the "per se" cause of one, and many are only the accidental cause of one, inasmuch as they are in some way one. Since therefore what is first is most perfect, and is so "per se" and not accidentally, it must be that the first which reduces all into one order should be only one. And this one is God. (ST I, Q. 12, Art. 3)

He adds in article 4 the supremacy of God's oneness,

> Since "one" is an undivided being, if anything is supremely "one" it must be supremely being, and supremely undivided. Now both of these belong to God. For He is supremely being, inasmuch as His being is not determined by any nature to which it is adjoined; since He is being itself, subsistent, absolutely undetermined. But He is supremely undivided inasmuch as He is divided neither actually nor potentially, by any mode of division; since He is altogether simple, as was shown above (Question 3, Article 7). Hence it is manifest that God is "one" in the supreme degree. (ST I, Q. 12, Art. 4)

Concerning the diversity in nature we can perceive with our senses, not least of which also concerns changes in nature subject to time, and which we understand from revelation as Genesis explains its creation, St. Thomas's explanation of the relationship between what is perceived and what is revealed may begin to be drawn. As St. Thomas writes,

> Hence we must say that the distinction and multitude of things come from the intention of the first agent, who is God. For He brought things into being in order that His goodness might be communicated to creatures, and be represented by them; and because His goodness could not be adequately represented by one creature alone, He produced many and diverse creatures, that what was wanting to one in the representation of the divine goodness might be supplied by another. For goodness, which in God is simple and uniform, in creatures is manifold and divided; and hence the whole universe together participates [in] the divine goodness more perfectly, and represents it better than any single creature whatever.[44] (ST I, q. 47, art.1)

---

[44] I, q. 47, a. 2. (Unless otherwise indicated, all citations from the *Summa* are from the translation by the Fathers of the English Dominican Province.)

1. Most of the information here is taken from Bertrand Russell on God and Religion edited by Al Seckel (Buffalo, N.Y.: Prometheus Books: 1986). Some information is taken from online resources and from The Autobiography of Bertrand Russell (Boston: Little, Brown and Co., 1951).

2. See Seckel, Bertrand Russell on God and Religion, p. 27)

3. Ibid., p. 22

4. Ibid., p.10

5. Ibid., p. 57

6. Ibid., p. 61

And further in the next article of that question, St. Thomas explains the reason for inequality in such diversity,

> [A]s the wisdom of God is the cause of the distinction of things, so the same wisdom is the cause of their inequality. This may be explained as follows. A twofold distinction is found in things; one is a formal distinction as regards things differing specifically; the other is a material distinction as regards things differing numerically only. And as the matter is on account of the form, material distinction exists for the sake of the formal distinction. . . . Now, formal distinction always requires inequality, because as the Philosopher says (Metaph. viii, 10), the forms of things are like numbers in which species vary by addition or subtraction of unity. . . . as the divine wisdom is the cause of the distinction of things for the sake of the perfection of the universe, so it is the cause of inequality. For the universe would not be perfect if only one grade of goodness were found in things. (ST I, q. 47, art.2)

A perfect being defined by his oneness, then, outflows diversity onto the world; and beyond St. Thomas's explanation of the reasons for diversity in nature, we also perceive diversity among human persons. If we are all created in the image and likeness of a perfect being, why are we also diverse in our talents, our gifts, our inclinations and in the many other ways

---

7. History of Western Philosophy (N.Y.: Simon and Schuster, 1945)

8. Ibid., p. 455 ff.

9. Ibid., p. 462

10. Bertrand Russell on God..., p. 65

11. Ibid., pp. 123-146

12. Ibid., pp. 131-132

13. Ibid., see p. 33

14. Ibid., p. 11

we might find diversity in us? St. Catherine provides in her *Dialogues* a strong explanation based on the fact that human persons are social beings. Our diversity requires us to come together in community, to learn to love one another for the complementary gifts each person brings, so that by our loving one another in community, we can better love God who brought us into being within community.

While God is One, God also has attributes of God that we can understand in relational terms. St. Thomas provides descriptions of these that follow from his demonstrations found in the five ways. These attributes are as follows concerning why God should create at all, and a good source for discussion of them may be found in Chapter 4 of Peter Kreeft and Ronald K. Tacelli's *Handbook of Christian Apologetics*, which deals with the nature of God.

Of those atheists who claim that they can wrap their minds around the idea of an intelligent designer but will never believe in the God of Scripture, they seem to be saying that a God who is remote and not intimately involved in their lives is fine, but not a God who is Lord of our Lives and who has laid out a moral framework as part of a plan to personally guide each and every one of us back to Him. Such a stance betrays a great deal of the persons who hold it. It shows that they do not think that one can prove, philosophically, that the God of the five ways also has attributes such as Goodness and Beauty. What follows, then, is a summary of the proofs of God's attributes from the great philosophers, especially St. Thomas Aquinas, as provided by Kreeft and Tacelli.[45] The point is that Sacred Scripture reveals that the God we can come to know by reason is the same God who has revealed himself to us in Scripture.

---

[45] Peter Kreeft and Ronald K. Tacelli, *Handbook of Christian Apologetics* (Downers Grove, IL: IVP Academic, 1994), 90-99.

God Exists Absolutely

From the proofs for the existence of God, we know that God is the source of all being. Now the finite beings we see around us do not have to be. There could be a world without, say, any pelicans in it. There is a difference between the essence of a pelican (what it is) and that a pelican exists (that it is). But God, by definition, the necessary being, exists always and does not simply happen to be, for all the other existents depend on God. There is no difference between the essence of God (who he is) and the existence of God (that he is). This distinction was expressed most succinctly by St. Catherine of Siena in her *Dialogues* when Christ explains to her, "I am he who is. You are she who is not."

God is Infinite

Finite, or limited, things require a cause, but God, who is the First Cause, cannot be limited, for otherwise God would need a cause;[46] consequently, he would not be that which we know as the uncreated God, but a lesser, created being. If that were the case, we would seek his Creator. Kreeft and Tacelli explain it in these terms: "People often think that by the infinity of God is meant immense size ... as if God were ... bigger than anyone could measure. But by saying God is infinite we mean that God is (free) of any limitation at all . . . God is the very fullness of being."[47] That God is infinite means necessarily that he is limitationless.

---

[46] Kreeft and Tacelli, 92.
[47] Kreeft and Tacelli, 92.

God is One

If there were many gods, none of them could be God because one would have what some other one did not have, or they would be identical and therefore the same. God as source of all has to be one. We understand the oneness of God from our faith, but we have also had the Holy Trinity revealed to us whereby God is three persons in one substance. The Cappadocian fathers—St. Gregory Nazianzus, St. Basil, and St. Gregory of Nyssa—explained this in terms of relationship among the Divine Persons. God the Father generated the Son, who is the Word, and the Holy Spirit proceeded from the love They share. The three Divine Persons are in this way one substance, distinct only in their relations to one another.

God is Spiritual

God cannot be a material thing such as the whole universe. To call the whole universe God would mean that the universe would have to peel off parts of its matter to make more matter. The universe is something full of change due to its motion and to motion's measure, which is time, but God is the cause of all motion, which means that he cannot also be subject to it or its measure. What is created by God, therefore, is not made up of pieces of God, as that would mean God would have parts. The Spiritual or Immaterial does not have parts but is self-subsistent being.

God is Eternal

There are two meanings of the word eternal: everlasting and timeless. Both are different from the idea of the temporal, which refers to beings who begin in time, at a certain moment, and end at death, the end of time for them. Everlastingness refers to beings who never stop moving through time after they are created such as angels and human souls. Timeless refers to God who, being Absolute, is never changing, eternal in this sense. Boethius, Kreeft and Tacelli defines eternity as "Life without limits, possessed perfectly and as a simultaneous whole."[48] Since God does not have a beginning, as shown by the Five Ways, God is eternal: timeless. "God cannot be a part of the universe. . . . God is the Creator of all things, giving them their total being. . . . So God must be other than the creation. That is what we mean by the transcendence of God. At the same time God must exist in all things. They cannot be set over against (God) for then God would be limited by them. . . . God is the Creator, the giver of the total being to all things. As such God must be active in giving them what they need to be and to act. If God were not actively communicating being to all things, they would cease to be. So God must be present to all things at their deepest core. . . . In other words, God is immanent."[49] Note how this affirmation of God's transcendence and immanence avoids the one-sided pitfalls of pantheism (which identifies God with material nature) and deism (which makes God remote from creation, as if he could wind it up and let it run on its own). Immanence means God is separate from nature but present to it and us.

God is Intelligent

This follows from the fifth Way of St. Thomas concerning design. "All the vast intelligibility, which the world is given by its Creator, is the work of intelligence, and therefore, the Creator is intelligent." Only a conscious and perfect intelligence can hold all being together as an artist puts everything together in his work.

---

[48] Kreeft and Tacelli, 93.
[49] Kreeft and Tacelli, 93-94.

God is Omniscient and Omnipresent

God knows everything about everyone and everything everywhere. "To say that God is omniscient and omnipotent means that there can be no real barriers to God's knowing or acting. . . . God has created everything there is to be known and sustains it in being. So is it conceivable that there is something he could not know or not have power over?"[50] Later in our chapter on the problem of evil (pain), we will explain how God may be all-loving and all-powerful yet allow evil in the world.

God is Good

God is the fountain of goodness. "God is the source of all that we recognize as good,"[51] and by that is meant good in the dual sense of the goodness of something as demonstrated by its being in existence at all and in moral goodness. "God is the source of all being; therefore, God cannot be evil in any way" as moral or physical evils are defects.[52] A thing is "bad if it fails. Now there can be no questions of failure on the part of the Creator; God is to the fullest . . . insofar as goodness is one with perfect being, God is perfect good."[53] God's goodness does not fail.

This philosophical analysis of the attributes of God in no way gives us the understanding Scripture does of the God of Love, but it helps us see revelation in terms of something that is not absurd. It helps us to recognize the dynamic possibilities of the connection. That should keep us from imagining that all we can prove is a God who is the source of everything but about whom we can know nothing whatsoever. That is to say,

---

[50] Kreeft and Tacelli, 96.
[51] Kreeft and Tacelli, 96.
[52] Kreeft and Tacelli, 96.
[53] Kreeft and Tacelli, 96.

it shows personality, and the concept of personality makes possible the concept of relationship. It is in the person of God, the Son incarnate, that we learn the most about what God the Creator, the Father, is really like. We may learn that the ideal father is real.

Taking God's Identity into Dialogue with the Atheists

Our bringing the discussion back to persons, then, enables us to talk about some specific theists in dialogue with atheists in light of the foregoing proofs and attributes. What emerged over the 20th century was a kind of battle for the minds of others as atheists sought to legitimize and spread their beliefs and Christian apologists sought to affirm theirs in light of the attack atheists launched against the faith. Atheists like Bertrand Russell were a product of many of the intellectuals of the eighteenth and early nineteenth centuries who believed in God but had doubts about specific teachings of their rabbis, priests and pastors. By the beginning of the 20th century, many young people of the educated classes had become either atheists or agnostics. Their questions had snowballed into disbelief.

One of the greatest atheists of the 20th century was Bertrand Russell, who subordinated everything to the altar of scientific materialism, the growth of which was greatly stimulated by Darwinist speculations. This makes Russell a kind of intellectual father to Richard Dawkins, whose *God Delusion* purports to have found the cause of all existence in the slow and gradual evolutionary process of material existence in the process of moving from one state of existence to another. After all, what is an impressionable young person to make of the apparent discrepancy between the Biblical view of creation and evolutionary theory if lacking in proper guidance concerning his or her faith? Of course, the Christian faith is more than plausible, but understanding is an exercise in study and reflection.

Brought up as a Christian, Russell would come to the conviction that the only things we can be sure even exist are those that can be known through the senses. Accordingly God, being by definition non-sensate, could not be proven or disproven. Among Russell's peers, God and the soul were considered mere figments of the imagination. It was thought that the only future for philosophers was to give up speculating about the meaning of the life and the universe and confine themselves to engendering criteria for evaluating scientific theories or problems stemming from language.

A famous example is the way that the twentieth century English philosopher of the school of linguistic analysis, Gilbert Ryle, tried to explain away the reality of our immaterial minds. Suppose someone had never seen a university. He visits. You show him the auditorium, the labs, the gym, etc., and he then says: 'all well and good, but where is the university?' He is making what Ryle called a category mistake in language, thinking the university is something different from its parts. Similarly, if you describe what the brain does, the mind is not something separate, as traditional philosophers thought, but just, according to Ryle, an overall word for the parts of the brain in action! What is lost is the understanding how the parts contribute to the whole—how diversity may participate in unity.

Bertrand Russell's story gives us some insight into how he lost his faith in a personal God. He was an orphan whose mother died when he was two and whose father died when he was three and a half. In his youth, then, he experienced great loneliness since his brother was older and was away in boarding school. Bertrand was very fearful he might never meet anyone he could talk to. He spent his youth less with people than with nature, books and mathematics. Russell loved Euclid and found mathematics an ecstasy! He disliked, though, the fact that you had to agree to axioms to proceed vs. questioning the axioms as well. Such thorough critique he would later accomplish himself in his famous book *Principia Mathematica* written with Alfred North Whitehead. In this book, he proved that mathematics is reducible to formal logic.

Russell's father was a free-thinker. His mother ran a philosophical salon. When his father died, he left two tutors for his sons who were instructed to be sure to protect the lads from harmful religious belief! After the death of that father, against his stated wishes, the court awarded Russell to his religious grandparents because they were part of the English nobility.

The boy moved to a large castle-like house and grew up not remembering what his parents were like. This is significant only in that some psychologists such as Karl Stern and Paul Vitz have noticed that quite a number of atheistic thinkers have been orphaned or otherwise separated from loving maternal influence.

Russell's grandmother, who loved him deeply, was a Presbyterian who became a Unitarian at the age of seventy. She was liberal in politics but extremely strict in morality. Her fearlessness, public spirit, contempt for convention and indifference to the opinion of the majority influenced Russell to be willing to belong to small minorities. Though Bertrand's grandparents took him to church, by about fifteen he started studying arguments for God, freedom and immortality, and he fell into skepticism. The first widely held belief he doubted was the existence of free will. He thought that if everything is caused by matter, then the will, which cannot be matter, could not have any influence on the body as in the will deciding to move your hand. The human body is a machine. Still he did not see himself as a pure materialist since he thought that consciousness itself was not material. By age seventeen, he doubted immortality as well. In his autobiography, Russell claimed that there were three passions that governed his life, longing for love, seeking knowledge and compassion for the sufferings of others.

Russell still believed in God since he thought that the Thomistic argument from causality was valid. Later on, thinking about the question of who made God led him to become an atheist. This process from doubt to atheism, the notion that there is certainly not a God took Russell a long time to reach and initially made him unhappy, but eventually he was glad to be done with the whole matter. Russell thought that since religious philosophy does not involve the type of evidence you have in science, theological ideas should not even come up for evaluation. As a young adult, Russell's skepticism led him into despair. The only reason he did not commit suicide in his loneliness was because he wished to know more of mathematics and did not want to hurt his grandmother. Many years later Russell wrote that society is in chaos primarily because there is so little Christian virtue left.

Going back to Russell's entrance into the life of the university, he soon realized that skepticism has consequences. What he had been taught to abhor as a Christian boy, now seemed virtuous. He saw he was being led into sin. Evolutionary ideas about having been descended from apes lowered his idea about human behavior. For a while he thought it better not to spread his skeptical ideas. A famous philosophical joke that was circulated in those days concerning abstract metaphysical subjects went like this: "What is mind? No matter. What is matter? Never mind." Another story which illustrates the academic mind of this period is an answer Russell got to a question he used to ask his friends: "If you had the power to destroy the world, would you do so?" This was to see how pessimistic people were. One of his friends answered in the presence of his wife and child "What? Destroy my library? – Never!"

As a professor, Russell fell in love with an American girl whose family moved to England. You must not think that there is a straight line from disbelief in God, or free-thinking as it was then called, and sexual sin. Russell reports that even though deeply in love he felt no conscious desire for sexual relations. He proposed without ever kissing her or even holding her hand. Both the husband and the wife were virgins. She was a suffragette and total abstinence speaker. Her mother was so radical a feminist even in those times that it is reported she disliked the Deity for being called "He!" In 1901 after seven years of marriage, Russell fell out of love with his wife. For nine years afterward, they still lived together. But eventually he fell in love with another man's wife and had an affair with her for many years.

A great theme for discussion at that time was whether one could be good without believing in God. Russell insisted one could. A list for how to be good in this way included tithing to the poor, abstinence from liquor, diet, reading poetry or spiritual reading every day, punctuality, tidiness. He believed in inner discipline over exterior discipline and total spontaneity.

Russell had a huge crisis when the wife of his great philosophical comrade, Whitehead, had a heart attack in his presence. Until then he had kept to matters of the intellect and had avoided deeper issues such as the meaning of death. Witnessing the heart attack Russell reported that within five minutes he decided that loneliness was terrible and that only a higher type of love such as religions preach could alleviate it. A yearning for immanent intimacy was kindled. He became convinced that any action not motivated by love was wrong such as war in the world and bullying in school. These reflections were followed by a longing to help children. When Russell did have his own children with his wife Dora, the couple opened their own private school. It did not succeed largely because of discipline problems.

During World War I, Russell was a pacifist. In 1916, he was convicted and fined for anti-war activities and spent 6 months in prison. He was always an individual thinker. It would be erroneous to imagine that he followed a liberal political line uncritically. For example, when communism was all the rage he rejected the socialist belief that the State was the answer to social problems. He saw how social theory led people to tolerate Soviet Russia, and predicted the horrors of Bolshevism. He thought that the eradication of suffering would have to come not from State programs, but from changing men and women to be more rational, cooperative and kind. In spite of general pacifistic attitudes, during World War II Russell thought war was justified since living under Hitler would be hell.

Russell married four times and had many affairs. Always interested in political matters, he ran unsuccessfully for parliament several times. He taught in the United States in the late 1930's at City College until his appointment was revoked on the basis that he was morally unfit because of his behavior with women.

Russell won the Nobel Prize in 1950. During the 50's and 60's, Russell was involved in anti-war protests and anti-nuclear protests and was imprisoned in 1961 for nuclear disarmament protests. He died at 97.

Russell described himself as a "rational sceptic" defined as "withholding judgment where the evidence is not sufficient, or, even more so, when there is contrary evidence." He considered religion to be in the main harmful and was especially against religious objections to contraception since he thought that world poverty and war could never be eliminated without contraception. Another remedy he favored was the killing of the sacred cows for food to reduce hunger in India.

In 1927 in an article entitled "Why I am Not a Christian," Russell tried to refute the traditional arguments from First Cause and from Design in these ways:

"If you ask who made the world then you would have to ask, who made God?

"If everything must have a cause, then God must have a cause. If there can be anything without a cause, it may just as well be the world as God, so that there cannot be any validity in that argument...There is no reason why the world could not have come into being without a cause; nor, on the other hand, is there any reason why it should not have always existed. There is no reason to suppose that the world had a beginning at all. The idea that things must have a beginning is really due to the poverty of our imagination. Therefore, perhaps, I need not waste any more time upon the argument from the First Cause.

"You all know the argument from design: everything in the world is made just so that we can manage to live in the world, and if the world was ever so little different we could not manage to live in it. That is the argument from design. It sometimes takes rather a curious form; for instance, it is argued that rabbits have white tails in order to be easy to shoot. I do not know how rabbits would view that application. It is an easy argument to parody. You all now Voltaire's remark, that obviously the nose was designed to be such as to fit spectacles...since the time of Darwin we understand much better why living creatures are adapted to their environment. It is not that their environment was made to be suitable to them, but that they grew to be suitable to it, and that is the basis of adaptation. There is no evidence of design about it.

"When you come to look into this argument from design, it is a most astonishing thing that people can believe that this world, with all the things that are in it, with all its defects, should be the best that omnipotence and omniscience has been able to produce in millions of years. I really cannot believe it. Do you think that, if you were granted omnipotence and omniscience and millions of years in which to perfect your world, you could produce nothing better than the Klu Klux Klan, the Fascisti, and Mr. Winston Churchill."

In Russell's *History of Western Philosophy*, he has this to say about Thomas' Five Ways. After the briefest of summaries, Russell lauds Thomas for the fairness of his way of presenting arguments of opponents. "These merits, however, seem scarcely sufficient to justify his immense reputation. The appeal to reason is, in a sense, insincere, since the conclusion to be reached is fixed in advance." Would Russell want to universalize such an observation? Would he think that belief that England is an island makes the evidence of the geography insincere? Russell thought that only those who accept Aristotle's metaphysics will accept the Thomas' proofs:

All of these, except from the teleology of lifeless things, depend upon the supposed impossibility of a series having no first term. Every mathematician knows that there is no such impossibility; the series of negative integers ending with minus one is an instance to the contrary. But here again NO Catholic is likely to abandon belief in God even if he becomes convinced that Saint Thomas's arguments are bad; he will invent other arguments, or take refuge in revelation.

Russell's critique illustrates that if one eliminates metaphysics, of course, one cannot evaluate metaphysical arguments. Such arguments purport to be about realities, not about mathematical symbols for them. For example, numbers such as two and four can be seen as mere symbols. As words they are surely symbols. But having two children or four children is not a matter of mere mathematics! There is a real (metaphysical) difference! What did Russell think about Christ? In the article "Why I am Not a Christian," he has some intriguing things to say, such as: "teachings such as turn the other cheek, give all you have to the poor, and judge not, were excellent, but these were the precepts least popular among Christians!"

Here are some more observations of Russell about atheism, taken from "A radio program on the Existence of God" with Fr. Frederick Copleston, S.J., the famous Thomistic philosopher, on the BBC radio in 1948:

> Copleston: Would you say that the non-existence of God can be proved?
> Russell: No, I should not say that: my position is agnostic.

During this radio talk, Copleston used a version of the argument from contingency to a necessary being. Roughly this proof insists that if everything in the world is dependent on something else, there could be no foundation for being without one absolutely necessary being: God. When Russell replied that the world could just be there without the need for a cause, Copleston responded:

> Well, the series of events is either caused or it's not caused. If it is caused, there must obviously be a cause outside the series. If it's not caused then it's sufficient to itself, and if it's sufficient to itself it is what I call necessary. But it can't be necessary since each member is contingent (dependent) …the proposition that the world is simply there and is inexplicable can't be proven by logical analysis.

Very quickly in that debate it became clear that Russell did not accept metaphysical statements at all, believing only in truths of fact and analytical propositions. What, then, do atheistic-agnostics like Russell do about the fear of death? He replied that whereas young men may be justified in feeling oppressed by the thought of an early death, being cheated of the best things in life, an older person would be ignoble to fear the end. His ego should be receding so that he is merged with the universal life around him, happy to think that his life goals will be carried on by others.

Asked what he would do if he had to meet God after denying His existence all his life, he replied:

"Why, I should say, 'God, you gave us insufficient evidence.'"

In evaluating the thought of Russell, it is important to note that his rejection of the existence of God and of Christian truth did not mean the rejection of all Christian values. Russell held onto the theistic legacy by insisting on some trans-cultural moral values such as social justice, concern for the poor, and desire to eliminate the horrors of war.

On the other hand, Russell's rejection of metaphysics and consequent rejection of a First Cause leaves his philosophy in limbo. Yes, there are moral values but how significant can these be if the universe and all human beings will die with no hope of eternal life? Without a source of perfect love from God, how can human beings love each other with the fidelity necessary for family stability? If perfect love is not the framework for existence, then for what on the spectrum ought we to strive?

Philosophers like Russell grew as a result of their convictions to doubt the existence of God altogether (both that which could be demonstrated and that which had been revealed) while philosophers like Etienne Gilson strongly believed in the God who has revealed himself to us through scripture precisely because faith is on a different playing field from doubt. Faith is an active response to divine revelation, and doubt is a privation of certainty. One can act in faith, but one never acts in doubt, and the reason is from Aristotle's *Nicomachean Ethics*, where he writes that "every art and every inquiry, and similarly every action and pursuit, is thought to aim at some good." When we act, we act toward the thing that we think is best, even if we have weighed the opportunity costs of pursuing one act over the next best thing we could be doing, so action is a positive decision, one that demonstrates that doubt has ended in action (even if one wonders after the act whether that act was the right act to pursue).

Faith provides a consistent context for action while doubt provides no consistent context; so the atheist has to lose his or her doubt in order to see him- or herself as internally cohesive. To lose doubt, the atheist has to embrace a positive value, and the theory of evolution provides just such a positive value in that it provides another context for faith (it provides the vehicle without the driver). This faith, though, is in the evolutionary process of created things, and even Darwin understood evolution as bearing within itself a teleology, or movement toward an end. The end of adaptation within the natural world dead-ends within that world, and natural happiness is the best that can be hoped for. Faith in God, though, enables man to transcend the natural world and seek a supernatural happiness in joyful communion with his Creator.

How does one shrug off the faith context into which he or she was born, though, in order to regress from a faith in a personal and loving Creator to faith in an impersonal process of evolution? The answer is by degrees. Consider that once militant Marxists taught that religion was "the opium of the people," a sort of drug to keep them content in spite of the horrific injustices they suffered. Most people thought Marxist dreams of a perfect society based on waking up the poor to the benefits of shaking off oppression through violence were off base. Just the same, they were often shaken by communist rhetoric about religion. Could it possibly be true the faith of their fathers was naive? Could religion actually be a brake on the progress of the human race, deflecting energy from the alleviation of poverty with soothing thoughts of the after-life?

Such difficulties with belief in God gained strength at a time when philosophical doubt about God was rampant at the universities. In previous centuries the traditional proofs for God's existence were presented as wisdom. In the twentieth century institutions of higher learning, those proofs were mostly presented as quaint notions of the "medieval" period, which was so called because it was a time in our history in between the time of antiquity when philosophy was pursued 'unencumbered' with divine revelation and the time of modernity when philosophy was pursued with the intention of separating it from 'divine revelation.'

The medieval period, then, was the light of synthesis between faith and reason, and it found its culmination in the moderate realism of St. Thomas Aquinas. What followed in the modern period was no longer faith – even in a personal God as Descartes demonstrated when he tried to fight the atheism of his day through establishing a philosophy of doubt on which to prove the existence of God. It did not work as he had hoped, and he influenced the enlightenment philosophers such as Hume and Kant, who carried the concept of radical doubt into an era of skepticism about any but scientific knowledge. Faith was relegated to the private sector while the public sector fell into material reductivism.

A highly influential philosopher directing the 20th century mind toward skepticism about God was Ludwig Wittgenstein (1889 –1951). Wittgenstein was an Austrian Jewish philosopher who was the leading light of what came to be called the Vienna Circle. He later was a professor of philosophy in England and was described by Bertrand Russell as "the most perfect example I have known of genius as traditionally conceived, passionate, profound, intense, and dominating." Wittgenstein inspired the philosophy called logical positivism and one of the foremost figures in the tradition of analytic philosophy. His most famous works were the *Tractatus Logico-Philosophicus* and the posthumously published *Philosophical Investigations* (1953).

What came down through the 20th century as the key concept of the logical positivists and the analytic philosophers is that the only knowledge that is certain is to be found in propositions that can be scientifically verified. Wittgenstein himself was rather agnostic based on the idea that since God's existence cannot be scientifically verified, it is fruitless to get involved in trying to prove or disprove His existence.

Another philosopher of the 20th century associated with skepticism was A.J. Ayer (1910–1989) author of the famous book *Language, Truth, and Logic* published in 1936. He was the leading English proponent of Logical Positivism. He believed that philosophy should get away from metaphysics and high-flown theories of all of reality such as those of Hegel, and concern itself, instead, with the analysis of the meaning of key terms, such as 'causality', 'truth', 'knowledge', 'freedom.' In ethics he is famous for his emotivist theory of ethics. In this, he claims that rather than asserting truths about absolute ethical norms, the asserting that something is good or evil, right or wrong, merely expresses one's emotions about those actions. Since proofs for the existence of God are based on metaphysical absolutes, philosophy should not waste time debating them. The very terms of the debate are meaningless, according to Ayer.

What were the theists doing about this frontal attack on the foundations of all religious belief? Often thrust into a defensive position in the academe, believers were challenged to meet the arguments of atheists and agnostics in a new, creative manner. A huge impetus was the encyclical of Pope Leo XIII entitled *Aeterni Patris* (read this if you have time – it takes about half an hour) concerning the renewal of Catholic philosophy. [54] This renewal was to be an antidote to the atheistic teachings flooding the universities. Catholic philosophers and theologians got to work reviving the perennial metaphysics, philosophy of being, of St. Thomas Aquinas. Foremost among such philosophers were the Frenchman Jacques Maritain and the French Canadian Etienne Gilson. With the revival of metaphysics, traditional proofs for God's existence could be defended effectively to refute the objections of contemporary atheists—though the audience of atheists often needed—and still need—to properly understand the dynamic possibilities of a realist metaphysics.

---

[54] Pope Leo XIII, *Aeterni Patris*, 1879, Available online at http://www.vatican.va/holy_father/leo_xiii/encyclicals/documents/h f_l-xiii_enc_04081879_aeterni-patris_en.html

Chapter 4: Science and Theism[55]

That science is limited is due to the fact that it deals with nothing more than material creation. Everything it measures, then, is only that which is manifest in some way within the realm of the senses. For that reason, science has no way disprove the immeasurable, no way to discount philosophy or metaphysical realities that are purely spiritual.

Science is not without its importance, however. What science can do is provide us with demonstrations of causality. Some effect lies before us as a fait accompli, and its very presence is suggestive of some causal agent that brought it about. Our own presence here is a case in point since the body, as Saint John Paul II has said, is the sign of the person. As material beings, we can identify in the presence of one another a material cause, but we are also spiritual beings created in the image and likeness of God, which means we can identify in our communion with one another a formal cause. Evidence of this, in fact, may be found our being persons of communion. "That man should speak is nature's own behest;" our great ancestor Adam is made to say in the eighth sphere of Dante's Paradiso, "but that you speak in this way or that/ nature lets you decide as you think best" (Canto XXVI, 130-2). The same is true with our science – that we pursue the mechanics of this world with wonder is in our nature; the manner in which we do it is up to us.

---

[55] This chapter was earlier published in *Toward a 21st Century Catholic World-View: A Course of Studies of the Holy Apostles College and Seminary Community,* ed. by Ronda Chervin (Corpus Christi, Tx: Goodbooks Media, 2014), 47-58.

It is far better to have a manner resonant with our nature than it is to have one that is out of joint with it. That is how this chapter addresses the question of Catholic realism – by showing that science and theism are mutually supportive of one another *when we understand their roles.*

"Science can purify religion from error and superstition; religion can purify science from idolatry and false absolutes. Each can draw the other into a wider world, a world in which both can flourish." Saint John Paul II, June 1, 1988, letter to Rev. George V. Coyne, S.J., Director of the Vatican Observatory.[56]

A millennium before Galileo, the Church had accepted this nostrum: that the book of nature and the book of Scripture were both written by the same Author, and they will not be in conflict when properly read and interpreted. Our new translation of the Nicene Creed confirms this, in part, where we say, "Creator of heaven and earth, and of all things visible and invisible." This visible world, according to Dr. Tom Sheahen, director of the Institute for Theological Encounter with Science and Technology, "is the world science can access, with microscopes and telescopes, etc. It occupies space and time and is made out of atoms. This is where sciences like physics contribute. But there is an 'invisible' part of creation, which has been revealed to us in Scripture. Humans have access to a portion of this. It's a mistake to think science comprehends it."

The visible and the invisible things, precisely because both were created by God, enable parallel and complementary paths toward Him. Concerning the visible things, Aristotle

---

[56] Available at http://www.vatican.va/holy_father/john_paul_ii/letters/1988/documents/hf_jp-ii_let_19880601_padre-coyne_en.html

wrote in his *Metaphysics,* "All men by nature desire to know. An indication of this is the delight we take in our senses." Pope Benedict XVI, in an address to the Pontifical Academy of Sciences on October 28, 2010, affirms the work of science in helping us to understand what is:

> The Church is convinced that scientific activity ultimately benefits from the recognition of man's spiritual dimension and his quest for ultimate answers that allow for the acknowledgement of a world existing independently from us, which we do not fully understand and which we can only comprehend in so far as we grasp its inherent logic. Scientists do not create the world; they learn about it and attempt to imitate it, following the laws and intelligibility that nature manifests to us.[57]

This provides the context for the transition to the invisible things,

> The scientist's experience as a human being is therefore that of perceiving a constant, a law, a logos that he has not created but that he has instead observed: in fact, it leads us to admit the existence of an all-powerful Reason, which is other than that of man, and which sustains the world. This is the meeting point between the natural sciences and religion. As a result, science becomes a place of dialogue, a meeting between man and nature and, potentially, even between man and his Creator.[58]

---

[57] Pope Benedict XVI, "Papal Address to Science Academy," October 28, 2010, available at http://www.zenit.org/en/articles/papal-address-to-science-academy.

[58] Pope Benedict XVI, "Papal Address to Science Academy," October 28, 2010.

Both the object of science—nature—and truth of religion are sustained by a Creator.

The potential dialogue that exists here between man and his Creator becomes an actual dialogue when man pursues his science by seeing the Creator as the cause of the created thing. Each new thing we learn, then, magnifies our understanding of the glory of God on whom we are able to gaze with increasing wonder at his sense of order, harmony, and design. The beauty of the natural world attracts us, and what is drawn toward beauty is drawn toward the reality of the person who made it. After all, while we learn about the world and come to know it through its effects, we do not create it; rather, it is created by God who knows Himself as its cause.

To begin to bring about an understanding of the relationship between faith and science, then, what is needed is a framework that advances the concept of causality, which Aristotle defines simply as that which brings something else about and is its reason for being. Aristotle explains that four causes exist, namely the formal cause, the efficient cause, the material cause and the final cause. The formal cause is the kind of thing something is. A cat, for instance, has a particular form that distinguishes it from a dog, and this form is predicated on the specific difference (the thing that makes something one species and not another). The specific difference identifies a thing's nature, so we can speak in terms of the common nature of a cat or of a dog. The efficient cause is that which initiates a thing's coming into existence. The study of an efficient cause is necessarily, then, the study of agency, of an identifiable being that brought something else into being. The material cause is the "stuff" of which something is made. The material cause of this chapter presently on the screen, for instance, is pixel and plastic. The final cause is the end for which something is made, the purpose, that is, of a thing. It is easy to identify the purpose, or a range of purposes, for any given object. Even if people differ on their understanding of a thing's purpose, they will agree that a given object in their hand has some purpose as demonstrated by their using it, as Marshal McLuhan demonstrated in his study of our technologies as an extension of our persons. Every person, place, event and thing (that is, all nouns) is explainable in terms of all four causes.

While the theist would say that the explanation of all four causes is necessary for all things, material reductionists consider only the efficient and material causes as valid. The materially reductive mentality, further, considers the efficient cause only in natural terms. A framework for refuting anyone, particularly atheists, who believe that only efficient and material causes are valid is to advance the understanding not only do we need to know that all four causes are necessary for a complete comprehension of a thing, but that we also need to know that agency, the efficient cause, is both a natural and a supernatural phenomenon. As far as our comprehending what a supernatural efficient cause might look like, it is helpful to think of it in terms of a Being who has in His mind the kind of thing He wants to create (what St. Thomas calls the exemplary cause, which is driven by His intellect) and the purpose for which he wants to create it (what Aristotle calls the final cause, which is driven by His will). We human persons, created as we are in the image and likeness of God, can also act as efficient causes. God allows, after all, secondary causes as St. Thomas explains,

> Two things belong to providence--namely, the type of the order of things foreordained towards an end; and the execution of this order, which is called government. As regards the first of these, God has immediate providence over everything, because He has in His intellect the types of everything, even the smallest; and *whatsoever causes He assigns to certain effects, He gives them the power to produce those effects.* Whence it must be that He has

beforehand the type of those effects in His mind. As to the second, there are certain intermediaries of God's providence; for He governs things inferior by superior, not on account of any defect in His power, but by reason of the abundance of His goodness; so that the dignity of causality is imparted even to creatures. (emphasis ours, ST I, Q. 22, Art. 3)

Or, more concisely,

God's immediate provision over everything does not exclude the action of secondary causes; which are the executors of His order, as was said above (19, 5, 8). (ST I, Q. 22, Art. 3, ad. 2)

In other words, by understanding the four causes and their spiritual repercussions, we have the opportunity to more fully understand the richness of reality, and our understanding provides opportunities to participate—in the co-agency offered by God to persons—in His perfect live.

Our establishing only these two things— knowledge of the necessity of the four causes and an understanding that efficient causes need to be thought of as both natural and supernatural—provides the frame of opportunity on which all other things may develop. The reason is that it allows us to then posit, for instance, that every physical object has a natural origin but that our cosmology points to a first, non-material cause, predicated by the question, where did the matter of which that physical object is composed come from? The question arises because all matter is contingent as evidenced by the fact that it changes. Any contingent being requires an agent, or causal being, to bring it about; and natural options, precisely because they are natural, can be only intermediary (not the ultimate)source of a thing's being.

Once we agree that a thing has an efficient cause that is also supernatural, it is not that far of a leap for us to understand that it has a final cause to which its form and matter are oriented so that all its causes work together in the realization of the thing's purpose. If we were to make a tool, we would do so with our end in mind, and that end would cause that tool to take a certain kind of form and be made with a certain kind of material so that its cause (its efficient cause) could create it for the purpose it was intended. It is no different with the human person who is created for a certain end (two, since a human person is made for both natural and supernatural happiness) and whose soul is so made that it can form a body from organic matter that has the capacity to glorify God with its life.

Following the trail of the four causes will lead us to understanding and happiness if we so choose.

Scholastic Science

The medieval period in European history can be characterized as having taken place between the age where the study of philosophy was unencumbered by Divine revelation and the age where the study of philosophy sought independence from Divine revelation. In that long period of philosophical scholasticism—stretching from the life of Anicius Manlius Severinus Boëthius (480–524 or 525 AD), who brought the philosophy of Aristotle into Christendom in his many translation efforts (one of which was Porphyry's *Isagoge*, an introduction to Aristotle's *Categories*, which provided the framework for Aristotle's *Physics*), to the death of St. Thomas Aquinas (1225-1274)—Christian philosophers sought to reconcile faith and reason.[59] Muslim philosophers,

---

[59] The length of this period is misleading, though. The next great scholastic effort made by the West after the death of Boethius did not

too, sought this kind of reconciliation in a period of activity extending from the life of Al-Kindi (c. 801-873) to the death of Ibn Rushd (1128-1198), and Islam called its pursuit in this area a Golden Age, and its catalog of accomplishments enabled, in part, the Christian European Renaissance.[60]

To advance the discussion to faith-supported advancement in science, the Islamic world during its scholastic period provides us with an excellent example of scientific advances guided by a theocentric worldview. By the time of the European Renaissance, Muslim advancements in science and technology had dwarfed those of Europe for four centuries. Christian Europe, on the other hand, pursued most of its scientific advancements following its scholastic period under an increasingly anthropocentric and materially reductionist worldview that slouched toward and finally fell into solipsism.[61] Robert Augros and George Stanciu address this

---

occur until the 12th century, the one that gave Averroes and all his great commentaries to the West.

[60] For a full treatment of this, see Jonathan Lyons, *House of Wisdom* (London: Bloomsbury Publishing, 2009). Other resources pertaining to this point include the following: Mirza Tahir Ahmad, "The Quran and Cosmology." *Revelation, Rationality, Knowledge and Truth.* (North Haledon, NJ: Islam International Publications, 1998). Available online at http://www.alislam.org/library/books/revelation/part_4_section_5.html; M.B. Altaie, "The Scientific Value of *Dakik al-Kalam*," *Islamic Thought and Scientific Creativity.* Vol. 5, No. 2 (1994): 7-18. Available online at http://www.muslimphilosophy.com/ip/dakik.pdf; Douglas Cox, "The Cosmology of the Koran" (2010). Available online at http://www.sentex.net/~tcc/quran-cosmol.html; Jon McGinnis, "Arabic and Islamic Natural Philosophy and Natural Science." *Stanford Encyclopedia of Philosophy* (Dec. 19, 2006). Available online September 1, 2011, at http://plato.stanford.edu/entries/arabic-islamic-natural/.

[61] A goal it accomplished in 1992 when the American Supreme Court adjudicated in Planned Parenthood vs. Casey that "[a]t the heart

Western worldview in their book *The New Story of Science* (1984) when they explain what they mean by the Old Story of Science, "that there was in the 17th, 18th, and 19th centuries the gradual building up of a world view in physics and cosmology that was progressively more materialistic" (p. ix).

The Muslims proved over a thousand years ago that a resurgence of an authentic intellectual tradition – one, that is, that pursues the relationship between faith and science – would benefit from a return to a strong faith tradition: for our understanding of created things requires a concomitant understanding of the ultimate source of their creation. This is not to say that we have not made significant advances in science and technology during the modern period (which in Church history is defined as the years between 1274 and the present day), but that those advances have not necessarily been oriented to our loving God with all our heart, soul, strength, and mind, or in loving our neighbor as ourselves (Luke 10:27).

In pursuit of the relationship between faith and reason, Saint John Paul II begins his encyclical letter *Fides et ratio* (1998), "Faith and reason are like two wings on which the human spirit rises to the contemplation of truth; and God has placed in the human heart a desire to know the truth—in a word, to know himself—so that, by knowing and loving God, men and women may also come to the fullness of truth about themselves."[62] As we continue through the second decade of

---

of liberty is the right to define one's own concept of existence, of meaning, of the universe, and of the mystery of human life. Planned Parenthood of Southeastern Pennsylvania vs. Casey. (1992). Accessed August 14, 2011, http://caselaw.lp.findlaw.com/cgi-bin/getcase.pl?court=us&vol=505&invol=833

[62] John Paul II. *Fides et ratio*. September 14, 1998. Accessed August 14, 2011, at http://www.vatican.va/holy_father/john_paul_ii/encyclicals/documents/hf_jp-ii_enc_15101998_fides-et-ratio_en.html

the 21st century, we find compelling reasons to articulate once again this relationship between faith and reason, and we can do this by reaching into the Western European intellectual tradition relying upon the method used during the Islamic Golden Age. One of the most compelling of these reasons is refuting—in a real way—the rise of the New Atheism that, according to Scott Hahn and Benjamin Wiker,[63] seeks the political power it needs to advance the culture of death identified in *Evangelium vitae* by Saint John Paul II.[64]

It is only when we have fully grasped this relationship between our theology and our science, indeed, that our arts will flourish with a truer purpose than they have long known— because if we do not understand what is and what ought to be then we cannot reflect upon what we intend to represent Philosophy, which at its core is the thought process of a human person contemplating the source of all created being, is necessarily a spiritual activity, for it is the exercise of the rational faculties, of the immaterial part of humankind. It is the very kind of activity, in fact, that enables us to transcend our material existence. For a philosopher to say that everything is material is, therefore, absurd: for in the very process of articulating that concept, the concept itself is negated. A proper philosophical anthropology is instructive on this point.[65] Essentially, the soul is a spiritual thing in a composite relationship with the matter that it forms.

----

[63] Scott Hahn and Benjamin Wiker, *Answering the New Atheism: Dismantling Dawkins' Case against God* (Steubenville, OH: Emmaus Road Publishing, 2008).

[64] John Paul II. *Evangelium vitae*. March 25, 1995. Accessed August 14, 2011, at http://www.vatican.va/holy_father/john_paul_ii/encyclicals/docum ents/hf_jp-ii_enc_25031995_evangelium-vitae_en.html

[65] To paraphrase C. S. Lewis, we are not "bodies," we are "souls" that form bodies; that is, our souls are the form of our bodies. *Mere Christianity* (San Francisco: Harper, 1952), p. 129. This is also what

To think that matter is "all that matters" is to limit ourselves significantly. It is to wear blinders and go as the driver of materialism dictates (and not to look upon spiritual things). If we are composite beings, then understanding spiritual reality brings about a particular way of looking at the world. We find, namely, that a relationship exists between material and immaterial things; and some immaterial things that cannot be known by our senses or our intellects and have been, consequently, revealed to us by a Person Who is our Creator. This is the essence of Christian theism, which is a faith seeking understanding, to quote St. Anselm.

If we are going to make headway on understanding who we are and what we are doing as we interact with the material world in which we find ourselves, we have, consequently, to approach our search for understanding in the attitude of faith rather than in the attitude of skepticism. What we want to do is reclaim scholasticism, not as defined through the lens of the Enlightenment that has informed so much of modernity, but through its own understanding of itself, an understanding that is apparent in what the Muslims did with it in terms of advancing the principles of science through the strength of their faith. We want to recover knowledge and methods that have been lost—to our great detriment.

The Catholic Church: Leading from the Front

In *The Phenomenon of Man*, Fr. Teilhard de Chardin, the priest who came up with the idea that one day our technologies would connect every one of us with one another

---

Statius explains to Dante in Canto XXV of the *Purgatorio* -- that the work of the soul is to form an operative body that can manifest itself materially within the material world. Dante Alighieri. (1308-1321). *The Divine Comedy: The Inferno, The Purgatorio, and the Paradiso.* Trans. by John Ciardi (1957). New York: New American Library.

for the purpose of strengthening our relationship with Christ, writes,

> After close on two centuries of passionate struggle, neither science nor faith has succeeded in discrediting its adversary. On the contrary it is becoming obvious that neither can develop normally without the other. And the reason is simple: the same life animates both. Neither in its impetus nor its achievements can science go to its limits without becoming tinged with mysticism and charged with faith.[66]

This realization, to mirror George Weigel's assessment of Saint John Paul II's *Theology of the Body*, is a kind of intellectual time bomb set to go off sometime during the 21st century as the chasm initiated by people like René Descartes that separated the pursuit of an understanding of the natural world from the pursuit of an understanding of the supernatural world starts to be spanned in the popular consciousness.

The natural world, after all, was understood by Aristotle and the scholastic philosophers who followed him to be the first level of abstraction, the level of material being where things like earth, fire, water, and air (in fact, all material phenomena – wood, for instance, and bricks) were manifest to the sensory perceptions. Anything that we can see, hear, feel, touch, or taste falls into the realm of this first level of abstraction. It is the realm that most of us understand because we can apply our senses to it in a meaningful way that allows us to develop a percept that can be transformed by our minds into a universal concept. We have to touch fire only once, for instance, before we get the universal concept of "hotness." After that experience, the sight of *any* fire will be a signal to us

---

[66] Pierre Teilhard de Chardin, *The Phenomenon of Man*, trans. Bernard Wall (New York: Harper and Row, 1959), 266.

to avoid coming into contact with it. When a child holds a magnet and attracts a paper clip, he or she "gets" the concept of attraction, that some things by their very nature are drawn to other things due to the nature of those things.

While the concept of attraction is highly applicable in the visible world, it is also applicable in the invisible world, which, was understood by Aristotle and the scholastic philosophers to be the third level of abstraction, that is, the level of immaterial being where things like God, angels, and departed human souls are not manifest to the sensory perceptions. This is the spiritual realm, the realm in which faith is required, faith, which Hebrews 11:1 defines as "evidence of things not seen; the substance of things hoped for." Because we cannot see them, the materialist would argue, they simply cannot
exist, and the kind of philosophical anthropology (like that of Sigmund Freud) that argues for the existence of a material soul denies any practical value of faith and hope (even to the point of sometimes excluding them analogically). The fullness of truth expressed in Catholic Realism is that we are drawn by love. We are attracted to it in a real and palpable way, and the source of that attraction is none other than God, the person who brought us into being for our own sake to live in eternal communion with Him. Our exploring the world that teaches us all sorts of things about its Creator which may even lead to the discovery of Him. And in the discovery of the Creator, we discover ourselves.

Scientific truths, of course, like philosophical truths, are not meant to replace articles of faith. They do, however, contribute to our praise of God. In 2012, Dr. Tom Sheahen did a short survey of a few advances of the past hundred years, the span of time put forth by Augros and Stanciu as "the new story of science," in an article entitled "Scientific Theories," which starts with the Jewish Albert Einstein, who did not believe in a personal God, qualifying what he did believe as follows:

My religion consists of a humble admiration of the illimitable superior spirit who reveals himself in the slight details we are able to perceive with our frail and feeble minds. That deeply emotional conviction of the presence of a superior reasoning power, which is revealed in the incomprehensible universe, forms my idea of God.

and ends with the Catholic Msgr. Georges Henri Joseph Édouard Lemaître:

In 1912, we had no idea of separate galaxies. There were some fuzzy objects out there, but telescopes weren't good enough to resolve what they actually were. Astronomy was still a fascinating field, but there was not yet a field of *cosmology*. Then along came Einstein's *General Theory of Relativity*, which was a comprehensive theory uniting space and time and gravity. Einstein's theory was totally different from what people had previously assumed. But Einstein's previous theoretical accomplishments (four important new theories in 1905) assured that many scientists at least paid attention. By 1918, a prediction of Einstein's theory was verified via an experiment conducted during a solar eclipse, and that greatly enhanced the credibility of General Relativity.

Dr. Sheahen's article continues:

Soon many more scientists got interested, because it was possible to associate the huge amount of observed astronomical data with a theory that made sense of it all. The measurable difference in light arriving from some very distant stars (the "red shift") provided convincing evidence that the universe was expanding – and that begged for an explanation. Einstein's equations of General Relativity involved *tensor calculus*, which was unfamiliar to most scientists at the time; but a few set out to solve those equations for special conditions of the universe. Einstein, who once said, "I want to know God's thoughts...the rest are details," himself believed that the universe was in a "steady state," hardly changing at all.

Around 1922, a Russian named Alexander Friedmann worked out a solution for a universe expanding from a singular starting point; unfortunately, he died soon thereafter and his work wasn't noticed. Working independently, Georges Lemaître, a Belgian Catholic priest, solved Einstein's equations for a universe starting at time t = 0 and expanding from a singular point to its present size. He turned that in as his doctoral thesis to both Harvard and M.I.T. in 1925, and that was quickly noticed in the western scientific world. When Einstein heard of Lemaître's work, he scoffed at it; and that disdain put Lemaître into an uphill struggle. The impression of a steady unchanging universe "out there" was very strong in those days, and the thought of everything starting off at a single point was incomprehensible to most physicists. Other critics sneeringly invented the phrase "big bang" to pile on the ridicule.

The disdain for Lemaître didn't last long. Better telescopes were built, and other galaxies beyond our own Milky Way were found. By 1929, Edwin Hubble's observations permitted a calculation of how fast the universe was expanding, and it was all consistent with Lemaître's theory. Einstein himself eventually came to agree with Lemaître – for the simple and honorable scientific reason that Lemaître's theoretical solution accounted for the data. Einstein's Theory of General Relativity, meanwhile, became fully accepted throughout the scientific world. With his scientific respectability secure, Lemaître moved in higher circles within the Catholic Church, and became a key scientific advisor to Pope Pius XII. In 1950, a most interesting backstage drama took place, which shows what real scientists think about even the best scientific theories.

Pope Pius XII saw that the big bang theory coincided very nicely with the narrative in Chapter one of the Book of Genesis, and was going to declare it to be true, a doctrine of faith. Obviously that would have been a huge accolade for Lemaître, a permanent vindication of his theory. Instead of rejoicing at this, Lemaître himself talked the Pope out of it. Lemaître explained that NO theory in physics, however elegant or reliable, is truly final. *Every* theory can always be revised; *every* theory can be contradicted (and thereby destroyed) by a single experiment. Lemaître knew his history well: only a century earlier, "the ether" seemed a sure thing.

In 1963, new evidence from radio astronomy gave further evidence that indeed the universe originated in a sudden explosion, and the competing "steady state" theory was abandoned. The big bang became the only game in town. However, with the passage of yet another half-century, recent observations have indicated that some correction may be necessary to Einstein's theory: there may well be some additional force (customarily termed "dark energy") that causes the expansion of the universe to accelerate. In the years ahead, will General Relativity or the big bang be corrected? Stay tuned.

It is enormously to the credit of Fr. Georges Lemaître that he stood up to sustain the independence of science and religion. Lemaître had an enduring confidence that both science and religion are complementary pathways to knowledge, but scientific theories can stand or fall on their own, and don't need religion to referee. As Albert Einstein said, "Science without religion is lame; religion without science is blind." More recently (1987), Saint John Paul II stated their complementary relationship very cogently: "Science can purify religion from error and superstition. Religion can purify science from idolatry and false absolutes. Each can draw the other into a wider world, a world in which both can flourish."

For the atheist and Christian alike, it is prudent that we keep Einstein, Lemaître, Pope Pius XII, and Saint John Paul II in mind—so that we may grow in truth and the meaning and purpose of truth.

Evolution

Of help to the discussions on evolution are two papal documents that discuss it. The first is the October 22, 1996, Address of Saint John Paul II to the Pontifical Academy of Sciences.[67] Note the fifth and sixth sections with their concern with dignity, metaphysical reflection, and the meaning of the person in relationship with God:

> 5. The Church's magisterium is directly concerned with the question of evolution, for it involves the conception of man: Revelation teaches us that he was created in the image and likeness of God (cf. Gn 1:27-29). The conciliar constitution Gaudium et Spes has magnificently explained this doctrine, which is pivotal to Christian thought. It recalled that man is "the only creature on earth that God has wanted for its own sake" (No. 24). In other terms, the human individual cannot be subordinated as a pure means or a pure

---

[67] Available online at http://www.newadvent.org/library/docs_jp02tc.htm

instrument, either to the species or to society; he has value per se. He is a person. With his intellect and his will, he is capable of forming a relationship of communion, solidarity and self-giving with his peers. St. Thomas observes that man's likeness to God resides especially in his speculative intellect, for his relationship with the object of his knowledge resembles God's relationship with what he has created (Summa Theologica I-II:3:5, ad 1). But even more, man is called to enter into a relationship of knowledge and love with God himself, a relationship which will find its complete fulfillment beyond time, in eternity. All the depth and grandeur of this vocation are revealed to us in the mystery of the risen Christ (cf. Gaudium et Spes, 22). It is by virtue of his spiritual soul that the whole person possesses such a dignity even in his body. Pius XII stressed this essential point: If the human body takes its origin from pre-existent living matter, the spiritual soul is immediately created by God ("animas enim a Deo immediate creari catholica fides nos retinere iubei"; "Humani Generis," 36). Consequently, theories of evolution which, in accordance with the philosophies inspiring them, consider the spirit as emerging from the forces of living matter or as a mere epiphenomenon of this matter, are incompatible with the truth about man. Nor are they able to ground the dignity of the person.

6. With man, then, we find ourselves in the presence of an ontological difference, an ontological leap, one could say. However, does not the posing of such ontological discontinuity run counter to that physical continuity which seems to be the main thread of research into evolution in the field of physics and chemistry? Consideration of the method used in the various branches of knowledge makes it possible to reconcile two points of view which would seem irreconcilable. The sciences of observation describe

and measure the multiple manifestations of life with increasing precision and correlate them with the time line. The moment of transition to the spiritual cannot be the object of this kind of observation, which nevertheless can discover at the experimental level a series of very valuable signs indicating what is specific to the human being. But the experience of metaphysical knowledge, of self-awareness and self-reflection, of moral conscience, freedom, or again of aesthetic and religious experience, falls within the competence of philosophical analysis and reflection, while theology brings out its ultimate meaning according to the Creator's plans.

The second is what the first directs us toward Pope Pius XII's 1950 encyclical *Humani Generis*[68] and its approach to evolution:

> 36. For these reasons the Teaching Authority of the Church does not forbid that, in conformity with the present state of human sciences and sacred theology, research and discussions, on the part of men experienced in both fields, take place with regard to the doctrine of evolution, in as far as it inquires into the origin of the human body as coming from pre-existent and living matter -- for the Catholic faith obliges us to hold that souls are immediately created by God. However, this must be done in such a way that the reasons for both opinions, that is, those favorable and those unfavorable to evolution, be weighed and judged with the necessary seriousness, moderation and measure, and provided that all are prepared to submit to the judgment of the Church, to whom Christ has given the mission of interpreting authentically the Sacred Scriptures and of

---

[68] Available online at http://www.newadvent.org/library/docs_pi12hg.htm:

defending the dogmas of faith. Some however, rashly transgress this liberty of discussion, when they act as if the origin of the human body from pre-existing and living matter were already completely certain and proved by the facts which have been discovered up to now and by reasoning on those facts, and as if there were nothing in the sources of divine revelation which demands the greatest moderation and caution in this question.

Much of the enmity between science and faith has at is core misunderstandings about both.

Conclusion

What we need to pursue is the restoration of the friendship between scientists and theologians who are both pursuing the same truth – the nature of the world in relation to its Source. For the materialist, that source is natural, and it dead-ends in the ephemeral material world. For the realist, that Source is supernatural, and it is God. Our science and our philosophy should point to the ultimate source of being, and we cannot find that in anything ephemeral – only in that which is eternal, in that which is God.

The relationship between faith and science takes an interesting turn in an era where New Atheists like biologist Richard Dawkins seem to be gaining ground in their fight against faith-based thinking. It may be important to remember that there was a time when Christian faith was not an issue in philosophy and science. Philosophers like Aristotle and scientists like Archimedes seemed to get along fine without it, each reaching the apex of achievement in their respective fields.

The question posed by the atheists and the New Atheists on whether our reliance on God somehow diminishes our understanding of our own value as human persons and our own capacity for intellectual acuity is really a non-question. We already know we are temporally finite because our bodies die over time, and we already know we are limited as evidenced by a myriad of factors, not the least of which involves failing memories and various incapacities in our ability to understand the fullness of the disciplines that lie remote from our own.

It actually increases our understanding of our own value as human persons to know that an infinite being, a necessary being, cared enough for finite, contingent beings such as us that He brought us into being in the first place and has reserved for us an eternal destiny in joyful communion with Him if that is our choice. It actually increases our understanding of our intellectual acuity if we know that the light of our understanding has a source beyond our own limited intellects toward which we can strive. Truth is a light by which we must choose to read the meaning of what is.

If we know that an eternal, perfect being created us and has a plan for our salvation, then the most reasonable thing to do is to rely on that being to provide us with the grace to achieve it. For this reason, we individual substances of a rational nature must cultivate an understanding of the relationship between ourselves and our Creator. Those of us who are not Pelagians have to ask ourselves the very simple question -- what good is the exercise of our Reason if it is insufficient by itself to save us?

The short answer is that Faith and Reason cooperate with one another in our understanding who we are – our identity – which is most perfectly revealed by Christ Himself who fully reveals mankind to himself. They are the two wings about which Christ spoke to St. Catherine of Siena as recorded by St. Raymond of Capua when He said, "You have two feet to walk and two wings to fly." With both these wings in flight, we are buoyed up by God's love.

Even so, we yet hit a limitation. As strong as we are created in the image and likeness of God whose natural law is written on our hearts, we need supernatural grace to perfect our natural gifts, and God provides it through the Holy Spirit who works within us. For us to gain by it, though, we have to consciously participate in the activity of God, in pursuing what Saint John Paul II called in section 41 of *Veritatis Splendor* a participated theonomy, since, in his words, "man's free obedience to God's law effectively implies that human reason and human will participate in God's wisdom and providence." We are lost otherwise and fall into wrath and rebellion.

Dante Alighieri is also of great help here as he makes explicit in his *Paradiso* that there are things in the mind of God that the created being cannot know. Though our hope lies in our salvation, God's mind is deeper than we can plumb, and that is a good thing because he shares of it with us is sufficient for our capacities. Dante writes in Canto XIX,

> In the eternal justice, . . . The understanding granted to mankind is lost as the eye is within the sea: it can make out the bottom near the shore but not on the main deep; and still it is there, though at a depth your eye cannot explore (lines 58-63).

While we have limits to what our science can do for us, we are not bereft of understanding. This understanding puts a new gloss on the relationship between faith and reason, between our faith and our science. We are at our best when we pursue our activities in full participation with the God Who created us with the capacity to do so, Who created us as creatures for our own sake, and Who takes delight in us when we pursue our desire to understand the nature of created things with full awareness that there is a Creator Whose mind has put all those things together. In the effort to advance a culture of life, after all, we must return to the work of understanding the relationship between our theology and our science. In doing so, we will find ourselves pursuing a new Golden Age—an age by which what is not yet understood will come to be so for the good of those persons who will follow after us.

Chapter 5: The Problem of Pain[69]

"Once again, the Darwinian must supply the explanation for why torture is effective; why we will do almost anything to avoid intense pain. Again it seems obvious to the point of banality, but the Darwinian still needs to spell it out: natural selection has set up the perception of pain as a token of life-threatening bodily damage, and programmed us to avoid it. Those rare individuals who cannot feel pain, or don't care about it, usually die young of injuries which the rest of us would have taken steps to avoid." (Dawkins, *The God Delusion*, p. 197)

Atheism champions a pain-free existence. But if atheism really were life-affirming, it should be as robust as faith is in the desire to preserve life– especially if this life is all there is and if the soul dies with the body. Instead, atheism tends toward pessimism. If there is suffering in this life, then it's fine to end the life in order to end the suffering. That is no way to live if one wants only to build character in order to live the life of the super-nice pagan, let alone, if one wants to dedicate one's life to any great or transcendent cause. We are more than our bodies, however. An animal's body is all an animal has, and it dies when its body dies; but a human's body has an immortal form, namely its rational soul, which was made for the purpose of the indwelling of the entire Holy Trinity.

---

[69] This is a revised version of a chapter in a book of Dr. Ronda Chervin's called *Tell Me Why: Answering Tough Questions About the Catholic Faith*, published by Our Sunday Visitor.

The atheist asks, then, "If there is a God of Love, why is there so much suffering in the world?" If it were only an ontic problem as Dawkins suggests, that we are simply programmed to avoid pain—and conversely, to pursue pleasure—then physical evil would be the end of it, and the far greater evil, namely moral evil, would not concern us. Furthermore, our desire to avoid pain would seem to lead to an equal desire to avoid inflicting it on others since we understand the damage it can cause. For this reason, the Darwinian solution is reductive precisely because it does not address our capacity to cause pain in others. On this particular position, the position lacks coherence.

We know that something beyond natural selection is at play here when our conscience informs us—as a result of our participation in the eternal law of God—that we have turned away from our Creator. We know that something beyond natural selection is at play here, too, when we reflect on the injustice that exists in this world. This question of suffering due to injustice is one that Habakkuk asks in the Book of Habakkuk 1:2-4,

> How long, Lord, must I call for help,
> but you do not listen?
> Or cry out to you, "Violence!"
> but you do not save?
> Why do you make me look at injustice?
> Why do you tolerate wrongdoing?
> Destruction and violence are before me;
> there is strife, and conflict abounds.
> Therefore the law is paralyzed,
> and justice never prevails.
> The wicked hem in the righteous,
> so that justice is perverted.

God answers him by saying that he will raise up the Babylonians as punishment for the wickedness of man wherefore Habakkuk complains a second time (1:12-17):

> Lord, are you not from everlasting?
> My God, my Holy One, you[c] will never die.
> You, Lord, have appointed them to execute judgment;
> you, my Rock, have ordained them to punish.
> Your eyes are too pure to look on evil;
> you cannot tolerate wrongdoing.
> Why then do you tolerate the treacherous?
> Why are you silent while the wicked
> swallow up those more righteous than themselves?
> You have made people like the fish in the sea,
> like the sea creatures that have no ruler.
> The wicked foe pulls all of them up with hooks,
> he catches them in his net,
> he gathers them up in his dragnet;
> and so he rejoices and is glad.
> Therefore he sacrifices to his net
> and burns incense to his dragnet,
> for by his net he lives in luxury
> and enjoys the choicest food.
> Is he to keep on emptying his net,
> destroying nations without mercy?

In short, Habakkuk is saying, "God, this whole mess is *embarrassing* for *you*. How are you going to fix it?" God replies a second time in 2:3-4 that

> the revelation awaits an appointed time;
> it speaks of the end
> and will not prove false.
> Though it linger, wait for it;
> it will certainly come

and will not delay.
See, the enemy is puffed up;
his desires are not upright—
but the righteous person will live by his faithfulness.

We, as people, are in need of perspective and understanding. We need the perspective in that what we see is so little compared to God who sees all and everything. We need understanding because we need to recognize that God has ordered the universe and that at the right time all accounts will be settled—all will be made right. Additionally, consider the parable that tells of the angels not removing the wicked so that the righteous will not be uprooted with them; it seems that there maybe be additional mercies present when injustices are not righted immediately.

Let us reflect in prayer with Habakkuk on this idea that "the righteous person will live by his faithfulness," as he continues in 3:17-19:

> Though the fig tree does not bud
> and there are no grapes on the vines,
> though the olive crop fails
> and the fields produce no food,
> though there are no sheep in the pen
> and no cattle in the stalls,
> yet I will rejoice in the LORD,
> I will be joyful in God my Savior.
> The Sovereign LORD is my strength;
> he makes my feet like the feet of a deer,
> he enables me to tread on the heights.

What is lacking in the atheistic understanding of pain and suffering is that of trust.

Here, we find resonant the words of Saint John Paul II in *Salvifici doloris* who leads with a question similar to what Habakkuk has asked, namely, why?

> Within each form of suffering endured by man, and at the same time at the basis of the whole world of suffering, there inevitably arises the question: why? It is a question about the cause, the reason, and equally, about the purpose of suffering, and, in brief, a question about its meaning. Not only does it accompany human suffering, but it seems even to determine its human content, what makes suffering precisely human suffering. It is obvious that pain, especially physical pain, is widespread in the animal world. But only the suffering human being knows that he is suffering and wonders why; and he suffers in a humanly speaking still deeper way if he does not find a satisfactory answer. This is a difficult question . . . man does not put this question to the world, even though it is from the world that suffering often comes to him, but he puts it to God as the Creator and Lord of the world. And it is well known that concerning this question there not only arise many frustrations and conflicts in the relations of man with God, but it also happens that people reach the point of actually denying God. (§ 9)

The question is not a problem for Saint John Paul II, though, for he already has the answer, which lies in the very faithfulness God uses to define a righteous person:

> In order to discover the profound meaning of suffering, following the revealed word of God, we must open ourselves wide to the human subject in his manifold potentiality. We must above all accept the light of Revelation not only insofar as it expresses the transcendent order of justice but also insofar as it illuminates this order

with Love, as the definitive source of everything that exists. Love is: also the fullest source of the answer to the question of the meaning of suffering. This answer has been given by God to man in the Cross of Jesus Christ. (§ 13)

We must ask those atheists willing to enter into dialogue to consider the cross as the solution to the problem of pain.

We lead out of the gate, then, with the fact that the question that has served as the greatest cause of doubt about the existence of God, namely, the reality of suffering, has already been satisfactorily answered. The atheist, though, who has not the light of faith that adequately addresses the problem of evil, still wonders how a good, loving God can allow so much pain when he could stop it immediately by means of his miraculous powers. Indeed, it is not only the atheist who wonders this but a good number of those who accept the truth of the Gospel message without fully understanding what it means in their lives. They hold what they perceive to be two seemingly contradictory realities, one in either hand, and cannot discern the means by which to reconcile them.

They look upon such baffling sufferings in the one hand as these:

- The death of infants.
- The destruction of whole communities in earthquakes, floods, drought and famine.
- Painful, lingering death caused by illness.
- A food chain that depends on each species devouring another species to survive.

And while they cannot comprehend the power and grace of the faith they hold in the other hand, they willingly endeavor to live within it despite what they perceive as an apparent contradiction to it. In short, they hang onto a faith they do not fully grasp by living in hope of a better world to come once they pass away from this one.

Some suffering such as that resulting from war, murder, abortion, incest, rape, abandonment, infidelity, theft, drug and alcohol abuse, to name a few, are clearly caused not by God but by mankind. A great portion of human suffering is caused by people (against whom we lock our doors and bar our windows at night) — certainly not God!

When we reflect on these evils, however, we tend to feel that there was a moment when God could have but did not intervene! "If only my child had left home two minutes earlier (stopped by God), she would not have crossed the path of that rapist!" "If I hadn't lost my good job (God could have changed the boss's mind), we wouldn't be living in the bad neighborhood where my son joined the gang that got him into drugs." "If I had gotten pregnant three months later, I would have met Joe and we would have gotten married and kept any baby we had."

The way C.S. Lewis, the famous novelist and philosopher puts this in his book *The Problem of Pain*, is like this: if God is loving and good he would have made his creatures happy, for God is by definition almighty, and an all-powerful God can do anything. But so many people are unhappy. Therefore, God lacks either goodness or total power (as Woody Allen jests: maybe God isn't evil, he's just an underachiever).

Actually, to get down to it, it is hard to understand why God created human beings at all. It is easy to picture a world of oceans, mountains, plants, animals, all just there flourishing but not needing to cause any pain — the world we usually imagine Eden was. It is when we add free-will characters such as angels and humans that the problem begins. It is the bad angel, Satan, who tempts man to explore disobedience and evil, and Adam and Eve who take him up on it. From that flow all the evils and more that we listed earlier.

Here, we come against fundamental philosophical and theological questions: why is there something and not nothing? Why did God create persons who can disobey him? Why did God create anything at all, for that matter, since he was happy in his goodness with just the Trinity for company?

Religious philosophers have racked their brains over this last one for many centuries. One of the best answers to be found is in the writings of Thomas Aquinas: goodness is naturally diffusive. What does that mean? It is the very nature of something good either to overflow or to create. For Jews and Christians, Scripture is our source of truth. The Bible tells us that God created. An analogy might help. Why is it that usually at the very peak of love between two people, when they feel most full, they start thinking of starting a family? Then after two children if not sooner, full of delight, they start thinking about a house, and maybe pets, and maybe more children. In fact, the greater their happiness, the more they want to create! Maybe God, who created us in his image, is like us in that way. Maybe he is so delighted with his creation that he planned for more and more.

Scripture tells us that angels and humans are the most like God because they are conscious, intelligent beings who can know and will and love as God can. Given the fact that angels and humans can disobey God and cause endless evils— should God have not trashed the idea of creating them? Well, consider the fact that when you dream of a child of your own, you know that this child will probably sin and also be the victim of sin. This thought causes some people never to procreate, but most believe it is worth it: that it is better to have life with at least some suffering than to have not life at all. Somehow they hope that the good in life and the good they hope for in an afterlife will make up for all the pain. Maybe God thinks that way, too. (It seems so!)

Such reflections may provide insight, but they never totally satisfy the human mind, especially when one is confronted with severe pain or when one sees loved ones suffering. In fact, suffering remains a mystery in the sense of never being resolved on this earth. Catholic Realism provides hope-part-one, but the second half will only be realized in Heaven—in the life of the World to Come.

But being a mystery does not mean that no light can be shed on it. The result of deeper and deeper thought is not so much to be convinced that there is no problem as to become convinced that it is right to love God, believing him to be good, even though it is not clear why everything happens as it does with such painful results.

Let us return to C.S. Lewis' philosophy in *The Problem of Pain*. Starting with the dilemma as stated above — namely that since God is almighty and supposedly good, he must be able to make us happy, not to live with pain — Lewis finds a solution in a close examination of the key words in this puzzle: almighty, good, and happy.

First, let's look at the concept of all-powerfulness. Many people get confused because they do not understand that to be able to do everything does not mean to be able to do what is self-contradictory. A famous old riddle goes this way: If God can do anything, can he create a square circle?

This question is actually absurd, for to be able to create anything does not mean to create a nothing. A square circle is really a nothing, because it is a contradiction in terms. There cannot be a square circle, not because God is limited but because it is an empty word — a non-entity.

Now, according to Lewis, the same analysis can be done with respect to the possibility of God creating a person (angel or human) who is free yet totally controlled by God! Since it is the very nature of a person to be free, a totally controlled person is just not a person but a robot.

What does this have to do with the problem of suffering? Well, consider the matter. Huge hunks of pain are caused by free-will decisions of humans, such as murders, thefts, wars and incest. It is Habakkuk's complaint. Now, if God simply waved a wand and destroyed the gun of the murderer, the hand of the thief, the bomb of the enemy, the organs of the rapist, how would these people be free?

It appears that given the choice of not creating any persons at all and creating persons whose freedom could hurt others, God chose to create us. Why? Augustine says because God can bring good out of evil. "Really? I don't see it," you might reply.

On earth we don't find justice, but in eternity God can make justice reign. There all our tears will be wiped away, promises Jesus. This means that an all-powerful God must allow for the possibility of the sufferings caused by evil persons as long as he wants to create persons at all. Would it even be worthwhile to create only robots run by himself instead? Would you rather have a robot than a friend, a child, a niece?

What about God's goodness? As Christ says, "No one is good--except God alone" (Luke 18:19). Here Lewis distinguishes between two meanings of good in our own human way of speaking. Sometimes by calling someone good we mean that the person gives us whatever we want. Other times we call good someone who gives us what is best for us even if there is pain involved. We may sometimes wish to think the dentist is an ogre, but we really admit with all the pain that he is good to put up with all our grimaces and shrieks and groans in an effort to help us retain our teeth in good shape. We may sometimes think that a friend who deals drugs is good because the customer wants these toxic drugs and will feel pleasure for a while after getting them, but we really know the drug dealer is evil.

Now it is clear that God is not good in the wrong sense of being one who gives us everything we want. One witty writer pointed out that if God gave all of us everything we ever wanted there would be no people left since at one time or another most of us wish at least one person would drop dead quickly!

But does God give us what is best? This is what we believe. We believe that he allows us to suffer because he sees that it can purify us! So, who needs that much purification? That is hard for us to see, especially about ourselves. In *The Problem of Pain,* Lewis penetratingly explains how much of our unfeeling indifference to others comes from not understanding their pain from within. The more types of suffering we endure, the more likely that we will relate to others with healing empathy.

Pain also weans us from the world. Since our true home is in heaven, it is not good for us to settle down to the temporary or partial joys and pleasures of what is only an inn on the pilgrimage. It is as if a child would only watch dogs on TV and never touch a real one. Real dogs might bite, but they are worth it. A kid addicted to TV might need to be forcibly pulled away from the set and persuaded to explore the real world. An adult addicted to the mixed pleasures of this world might need some goad to look upward at unimaginably greater sources of happiness, such as union with God.

Kahlil Gibran writes in the famous book *The Prophet,* "Your pain is the breaking of the shell that encloses your understanding. And could you keep your heart in wonder at the daily miracles of your life, you would accept the seasons of your heart, even as you have always accepted the seasons that pass over your fields. And you would watch with serenity through the winters of your grief." Winters prepare the ground for spring—and for the Christian, grief prepares the heart for the eternal spring, Heaven.

This brings us to the last word Lewis analyzes: happiness. By happiness some people mean a feeling of contentment, pleasure, absence of pain. Another meaning of 'happy' is 'joyful and hopeful.' Obviously, God does not keep us content in this life on earth. But that does not mean that all is

171 | C a t h o l i c   R e a l i s m :   a   F r a m e w o r k   f o r   t h e
R e f u t a t i o n   o f   A t h e i s m   a n d   t h e   E v a n g e l i z a t i o n
o f   A t h e i s t s

misery. He gives us joy that is not lasting, and hope in everlasting joy for eternity.

Here is a thought exercise you might do to understand this distinction better. Someone invents a miracle drug. Shoot it into your arm and you will never experience pain again. On the other hand, it will numb you in such a way that you cannot make any decisions or carry out any fresh actions. You will just sit in a corner smiling and content for the rest of your life! Would you take it?

At first, it might sound good, especially if you are in physical, emotional or spiritual pain at the moment. After a while, though, most human beings would rather put up with a mixture of pain and delight coming with freedom, especially if they anticipate a time in the future when all will be not numb pleasure but real delight caused by the presence of beauty, loved friends and God himself.

In this way, we can see that a real God of love does not create robots to avoid the pain that comes with our sin. He gives what is best rather than what is wanted and postpones our happiness, giving glimpses of it through occasional joys. Consider the beloved Psalm 23, popularly called "The Lord Is My Shepherd." The shepherd does not provide a giant insurance policy; rather, he is our Savior who is with us in the valley of the shadow of death that he himself endured, and who will lead us ultimately into the green pastures of eternal happiness. As a matter of fact, even an insurance policy does not guarantee that your house will not burn down, but only that you will be compensated later in the event that it does.

A careful reader will not be satisfied yet. What about all that suffering that comes not from free-will decisions of angels and humans but from nature? Couldn't God have made nature without any painful aspects to it?

Lewis came up with an intriguing insight here also. He claims that to have free-will creatures with bodies (such as humans), there has to be some kind of natural background. A body needs food, shelter and clothing. Now, a piece of rock honed sharp enough to cut can also pierce the skin of someone you want to murder. The natural being, the rock, is not at fault; it is our free will that uses it wrongly. The rains that are necessary for crops to grow can become floods. Earthquakes needed to restore balance to huge underground plates can also destroy houses—this is an ecologically framed answer.

Some present-day economists point out that many old tribal customs are the result of individual tribes preparing for all eventualities (such as drought and flooding) by storing necessities. The terrible sufferings of nations nowadays come largely, according to these students of society, from inequitable and inefficient ways of distributing wealth brought on by modernization. For instance, peoples who stop growing beans and rice in order to specialize in strawberries and asparagus for exportation to richer countries usually find themselves lacking in necessities in times of drought. We have the technology to rush emergency aid to any nation on earth, but we often lack the will to organize distribution effectively.

Theologians add that with the fall of mankind into original sin, nature fell as well, as understood in the famous passage of St. Paul where he tells of all "creation ... groaning ... [for] the coming of the redemption of our bodies" (Romans 8:22-23). All creation includes the animal kingdom, which fell because of mankind.

And yet, and yet, and yet ... that much pain? Do we need that much pain? Lewis himself had to ask that question when his beloved wife died of cancer. Suddenly, all his arguments in *The Problem of Pain* seemed meaningless to him. His grief was so great that he began to imagine that, after all, God might be some demon torturing us. Like Job of the Old Testament he wished that he himself were dead: "Why give life to those bitter of heart, who long for a death that never comes?" Ultimately, Job was saved from despair not by reasoning but by the overwhelming experience of the presence of God. So, too, did Lewis slowly gain strength not from his own reasoning, but from God's grace.

In the concentration camps of the Nazis, some Jews such as Viktor Frankl, were able to find meaning in suffering, a meaning that eventually brought him years afterward to belief in Christ. The Protestant woman Betsie Ten Boom, who was tortured in the camp for having hidden Jews in her house in Holland, told those in despair of God's love: "If you know Jesus, you don't have to know why."

Ultimately, Catholics believe as Betsie Ten Boom that it is the sufferings of Jesus on the Cross that stand as a mute answer to all those who would deny God because their pain has been so great. The voluntary suffering of the God-made-man proves that God does not watch our pain from a distance, wondering if we will keep a stiff upper lip through it all. No! God himself came to earth to show that in his love he shares our suffering and wants to bring us to the only place where there will be no more pain, only joy. What does the ticket to that "magic kingdom" cost? Only that our horror of suffering may help us to try to alleviate it, following the guidance of Jesus, the Savior.

What about the evils caused by theistic religious believers? I find that if the answers given about God's love and the pain in the world give atheists pause, then some of them immediately "fight back" by pointing to the evils caused by people who profess a belief in God and, further, profess their belief in a personal God with whom they have a relationship. They think that most of the wars in the world were fought by differing religious groups. Others think of religions as run by leaders eager to exploit the poor for their own benefit.

To deal with such issues we need to go into some historical details. Before doing so, however, it is good to bear in mind that billions of religious people have attributed the good that they do, day in and day out, to their belief in God and to God's helping graces. Why would atheists ignore all this good to concentrate only on evils? They seem to seek the privation of the good in order to advance the idea that a lack in something is not the exception to the rule but the negation of that rule. Saint John Paul II has a response to that, though, which reads in *Salvifici doloris*,

> Thus the reality of suffering prompts the question about the essence of evil: what is evil? This question seems, in a certain sense, inseparable from the theme of suffering. The Christian response to it is different, for example, from the one given by certain cultural and religious traditions which hold that existence is an evil from which one needs to be liberated. Christianity proclaims the essential *good of existence* and the good of that which exists, acknowledges the goodness of the Creator and proclaims the good of creatures. Man suffers on account of evil, which is a certain lack, limitation or distortion of good. We could say that man suffers *because of a good* in which he does not share, from which in a certain sense he is cut off, or of which he has deprived himself. He particularly suffers when he ought"—in the normal order of things—to have a share in this good and does not have it. Thus, in the Christian view, the reality of suffering is explained through evil, which always, in some way, refers to a good. (§ 7)

On the last assertion, Jesus himself seems to have given a partial answer in Mark 14:3 when some asked why a costly perfume was being poured out on his head when the perfume could have been sold and the money given to the poor. Jesus replied that the poor are always with us, but that this was something special since the woman pouring the perfume was anointing his body in preparation for its burial. Privation, in fact, points to the reality of the existing thing, after all.

Traveling around the world and visiting beautiful cathedrals, one is not given the impression that the people of the towns and cities think of the cathedral as something belonging to the priest or bishop or the pope. Rather, they regard the church as theirs. Poor as they may be, they can, if they wish, visit daily their "spiritual living room," reflecting the glory of the life to come in heaven.

This attitude might be compared to the way a poor married woman might cling to the gold ring on her finger as the last thing she would sell even to provide necessities. The ring symbolizes for her how important the bond of love is, even more important than the "daily bread," which would in any case disappear within a relatively short time after the sale of her treasure.

Great Church architecture, art, music, vestments, chalices, lace altar clothes — all these indicate that though social justice is important, beauty is also a hunger of the human soul. "One does not live by bread alone" (Matthew 4:4). Beauty may remind us that our suffering may be lifted up.

Among those who became Catholics knowing full well the evils of particular Catholics in history, some of the most striking conversions are of Jewish people. Realizing that Jesus, Mary, Joseph, the apostles and most of the early disciples were Jewish, they are thrilled to complete their Jewish heritage by accepting their Messiah and his Church.

Of more recent European Hebrew-Catholics, we have Saint Edith Stein, Venerable Francis Libermann, Raissa Maritain, Venerable Hermann Cohen, Max Picard, John Osterreicher, Father Alphonse Ratisbonne, and Rabbi Israel Zolli. From the United States, among the most well-known are Karl Stern, Father Raphael Simon, Charles Rich, and Father Arthur Klyber. Father Elias Friedman is a South African who was a Carmelite monk at Mount Carmel near Haifa in Israel.

He is the founder of the International Hebrew Catholic Association.[70]

Of those converts with a burning desire to help the poor who chose to work within the Church rather than to scorn her as unworthy, the one who stands out the most in our century might be Dorothy Day, founder of the Catholic Worker movement. At the time of her youth in the early part of the twentieth century, Dorothy had joined the Communist party hoping that social revolution could accomplish the justice that could not be found in the United States as it was. Disillusioned, she began to experience within herself a great spiritual thirst.

When she met the Catholic radical Peter Maurin, together they founded a sort of Catholic communism. They would champion the rights of workers as well as tend to the immediate needs of the poor by means of a newspaper, soup kitchens, hospitality houses and common prayer. They, like every Catholic saint, were concerned with active works to help the poor—to alleviate pain and suffering--and felt frustration because of the apathy of some middle-class and rich Catholics toward the desperate needs of the poverty-stricken. The response of the saints, however, was not to abandon the Church but to take upon themselves the task of instituting programs for the relief of the poor by supplying food, clothing and shelter as well as free hospitals, schools, and the like. The response has been that of St. Katherine Drexel who asked Pope Leo XIII what he was going to do for the poor in her area and received the reply that she followed, "Why don't you become a missionary?"

---

[70] For information about these and other Jewish converts to the Catholic faith see *The Ingrafting* (New Hope, Ky.: Remnant of Israel, 1987) and *Bread from Heaven*, available from the Association of Hebrew Catholics. *Honey from the Rock* edited by Roy Shoeman has other wonderful stories.

A model of how anger at apathy toward pain and suffering can become zealous service—transformation—can be found in St. Vincent de Paul of France who organized such rich ladies as St. Louise de Marillac to go out into the streets and find the orphans, the sick, the illiterate and help them. St. Mother Teresa of Calcutta's Missionaries of Charity has helped thousands of the poorest of the poor as do Catholic charities throughout the world. While working for social justice, we must offer immediate aid to reach immediate needs

What, then, about religious people persecuting others or leading Crusades? For some observers there is no organization in the world with a worse record than the Catholic Church! The very words "Roman Catholic," far from conveying images of great saints, remind such critics of tales of persecutions, inquisitions, religious wars, scandalous popes of the past and despicable priests of the present.

How could a church devoted to following the teachings of the Prince of Peace be so violent? How could followers of a Savior who was so pure give in so frequently to sexual sin? How could disciples of a Master who lived so poorly luxuriate in palaces?

The earliest history of believers in Jesus was marked not by sins of violence perpetrated by Christians but by martyrdom of Christ's followers at the hands of others. It was only when Christians became politically powerful that they were in a position to resolve disputes by force of arms.

Some wars were defensive and were waged against barbarian invasions; others involved battles over religious ideas. When there was a conflict between groups professing differing ideas about the nature of the Trinity or about Christ, and each group included powerful political figures, the situation was ripe for attempts to enforce unanimity through violence!

Eventually, many thought that if Church leaders themselves were chosen from the upper governing classes, greater harmony between Church and state would prevail. It was not long before one could find bishops and popes of little or no piety, chosen for political reasons.

It has always been a temptation for religious leaders of all faiths to seek the help of the state in the promotion of religious institutions. The results can sometimes be ruinous, for temporal power always tends to corrupt. Here is an example from our times: many religious colleges want federal aid for their students. But to retain this aid, they often believe they must secularize their schools by omitting prayer from classes not directly about theology, or by tolerating dissenting forms of pluralism to avoid any possible charges concerning lack of academic freedom. You might note that contemporary examples of worldly reasoning often seem less shocking than those of the past because our own compromises fit our cultural mind-set and therefore seem readily forgivable!

At the worst times of the past, elections of popes took months and even years as outside forces tried to poison the food of candidates deemed unlikely to further the selfish projects of princes and emperors. Other abuses included nepotism (handing out Church offices to nephews and other relatives in order to benefit the extended family in financial ways and also ensure allies) and simony (selling of holy things such as indulgences).

Although such practices seem foreign and almost bizarre to moderns, a close reading of Church history makes it easy to see how they developed from innocent to evil—to become vehicles of pain and suffering. To translate into contemporary life, let us suppose you were president of the United States. What would be more natural than to put into your cabinet a young nephew who was politically ambitious as well as good? This could easily lead to other members of your extended family expecting similar opportunities even if they were not especially suited for the posts in question.

Or, suppose you are a priest eager to renovate your parish church. Your flock is eager to participate through contributions, but you still need a little more to purchase the marvelous organ you saw on sale a month ago. Would it seem so evil to tell the congregation that you will say special prayers for the dead in those families who contributed more than one hundred dollars to the fund? It might seem like a bright idea until you realize that it could lead later to greater and greater abuses such as in the case of the lavish works of art found in great cathedrals now admired even by those Protestants (originally, protesting Catholics) who were so rightfully horrified by the sale of indulgences for the building of cathedrals at the time of the Reformation!

Happily, in our times, popes have little worldly power and the last century and a half have seen one holy pope after another. The story of the Crusades is also a sad one. There is documentation to prove that Church leaders planned these excursions for holy reasons. They believed that if the warlike knights could be sent to rescue the Holy Land from Muslims they would cease their local feuding. The knights of the Crusades were taught to avoid all unnecessary bloodshed and certainly to avoid the sins of looting and rape so prevalent in medieval times as well as in modern times. Unfortunately, most of the crusaders fell into the temptation of indulging in atrocities in spite of all warnings to the contrary. Wars, whether religiously motivated or not, always include atrocities.

It is contrary to fact to think that most wars come from religious conflicts. Countless millions of deaths came from massacres based on atheistic utopianism such as those perpetrated by Mao of China or the equally countless millions of deaths came from Stalin's atheistic Communism.

Indeed, a close reading of the Holy Scripture reveals how the chosen people repeatedly rejected the covenant and sank into immoral practices that caused many people much unnecessary suffering. Cycles of fervor followed by commitment to God and then by betrayal, punishment, repentance and reform are also characteristic, alas, of the history of all churches.

Of all the sins of people belonging to the Catholic Church the ones most distressing to potential converts concern the relationship of Catholics and Jews. In the early days of the Church, Christian Jews were afraid of Jews who had not accepted Jesus as the Messiah.

Later on, more and more Gentiles became Christians. As the Church became more powerful in the Roman Empire during the reign of Constantine, Catholics would often see the Jews among them as potential enemies — people not united by belief in Christ who might form an alliance with the enemies of Catholic emperors and kings. Living often in separate areas of cities, partly because they themselves wanted to be with kinsmen, Jews would sometimes become objects of envy if they were rich and subjected to violence by those wanting to steal their goods.

Most terrible was the way greedy Catholics and other Christians would time their looting and killing to coincide with religious holidays that could be used as a pretext for their riotous attacks on Jews. Based on the passages in Scripture about Caiaphas handing Jesus over to the Romans for crucifixion, irrational Catholic and Orthodox rabble would rush out of church on Good Friday to persecute and even kill innocent Jewish people. Such pogroms continued well into the twentieth century and have left an enduring mark of fear even in the hearts of Jews who have never known persecution personally.

Other forms of persecution and intimidation of Jews by Catholics had to do with political motives linked to religious issues. For example, in Spain where many Jews lived for centuries in prosperity and peace, the situation changed dramatically during the centuries of Muslim incursions into southern Spain. In those times it was feared that Arabs would take over all of Europe.

Mounting a holy war, or crusade, against the Muslims, the Spanish royalty such as Ferdinand and Isabella needed to be sure of the loyalty of all peoples in their kingdom. Could they count on the Jews? They were not sure. They worried particularly about the Marranos — Jews who converted to the Catholic faith, some because of a religious conversion to Christ but others purely as a defensive political move to consolidate their position in society. These practiced Judaism secretly in their homes.

It was not irrational to think that such phony converts might join forces with Muslims in a crisis if they thought it in their best interests. Since Isabella and Ferdinand actually favored Jewish converts as members of their court, it became critical to find out which converts were loyal and which shaky.

A way to decide appeared in the form of the inquisition. Set up to deal with Christian heretics, it was originally designed to protect the innocent by means of theological questioning by trusted Dominican theologians who were to substitute rational means for the type of torture so prevalent in all states at that time. The Church was not to be involved in punishment but only in making a judgment as to whether a person was heretical or not. Since heresy was deemed not only a danger to the Church but primarily to order in the state (that is, treason), in that heretics set up rival groups in collusion with foreign princes, it would be up to the state to punish the heretic.

Our most vivid image of the link between political factors and religious judicial procedures can be found in the trial and death of Joan of Arc. Even such unbiased chroniclers as George Bernard Shaw and Mark Twain, certainly not predisposed toward the Catholic Church, show in their portrayals how the real issue was not Catholic doctrine but political factors pitting the French allies of the invading English against loyalist French.

Going back to the Spanish inquisition, it was fear of internal traitors that led Isabella and Ferdinand to employ Dominican priests to determine which Jewish converts were sincere, with subsequent torture, death or banishment of the insincere. There is evidence that figures about the number of Jews burned at the stake are highly exaggerated, having been written up by a disaffected ex-Catholic and then quoted ever since to blacken the record of Church practices. But even so, the picture remains terrible and terrifying—Christianity gone backwards

Religious wars between Protestants and Catholics were common in the sixteenth and seventeenth centuries. Many of these wars were political more than religious. A prince who wanted to get out from under the temporal power of the pope had only to become a Protestant to acquire all the property of the Catholic Church in his lands. If there was resistance, this would lead to warfare. To people of the United States deeply imbued with ideals of religious tolerance, such wars seem incredible.

Even though we also have quite a history of persecution, particularly of Native Americans and African-Americans as well as Catholics, never have we seen anything resembling the Thirty Years' War in Europe from 1618 to 1648. Some of us view with disgust the battles going on between Protestants and Catholics in Northern Ireland, imagining they are fighting only because of distaste for each other's religion. Such is not the case. Economics and politics are the key to the violence. Religion merely parallels the long-standing inequalities in that country. It should be noted that the Irish Republican Army has many times been condemned and its members excommunicated by the Catholic Church for its vengeful violence. Similar action has not been taken against the gunmen on the other side.

Of course, whenever a nation is convinced that its wars are just, its citizens do not think of themselves as violent. In the past century, we in the United States were in almost constant war that has carried over to the present day: World War I, World War II, Korea, Vietnam, Panama, the Gulf War, Iraq, and Afghanistan

In the past century, the Nazi Holocaust, attempting to rid the whole world of its Jews, has been seen by many as a travesty rooted in previous religiously motivated anti-Semitism. No matter how much documentation we have from Jewish sources of heroic self-sacrifice in the efforts of some Protestants and Catholics to save Jews, it still remains true that many Christians preferred to save themselves than to reach out to those in terrible danger. This should not surprise Catholics of our time, for how many are willing even to peacefully picket an abortion clinic at no risk whatsoever? If this is true, how harshly should those be judged who to help Jewish neighbors during World War II would have ended up going to a concentration camp to their deaths?

It is important to read some of the documentation available about those whom the Jewish survivors of World War II call "the righteous of the nations," that is, those non-Jews who did risk their lives to help. Many members of the Catholic Church hierarchy roused the people to resist Nazism. The man who was to become Pope John XXIII forged thousands of baptismal certificates to enable Jews to escape to Israel via Bulgaria were he was papal nuncio. A booklet entitled *Pius XII's Defense of Jews and Others: 1944-45* by Robert R. Graham, S.J. (published by the Catholic League for Religious and Civil Rights, Milwaukee; longer version — *Pius XII and the Holocaust: A Reader* by Robert A. Graham and Joseph L. Lichten, also by the same publisher), addresses itself specifically to refuting the charges made by some against Pope Pius XII that he was negligent in defending the Jews, whereas in fact he worked tirelessly underground to save as many as possible.

Here is one of many telling quotations:

In 1937, when leaders of the Western democracies were scurrying to Munich to negotiate with Hitler, the Holy See condemned the theory and practice of the 'Nationalist State' in the encyclical Mit brennender Sorge [To the bishops of Germany: On the Church and the German Reich]. When Jews felt the cruel sting of Nazi hatred, the German bishops protested, 'Whoever wears a human face owns rights which no power on earth is permitted to take away,' echoing Pius XI's declaration, 'We are all spiritual Semites.' . . . While Britain and the United States were refusing to admit refugees to their territories, the Holy See was distributing thousands of false documents — life-saving passports to freedom — to the beleaguered Jews. . . . Catholic priests, nuns and lay people were hiding Jews in their flight to safety, and often paying for it with their lives. ... It could be asked whether these good works (praised by many European rabbis) were enough, whether it would have been better for the Pope to have denounced from the rooftops the crimes that were occurring. This thought troubled Pius XII, and he confided afterward to an associate, 'No doubt a protest would have gained me the praise and respect of many,' but he believed that such protest would only have led to more deaths whereas underground work would save lives.[71]

Does all of this miserable history add up to a proof that the Catholic religion leads people into bigotry, persecution,

---

[71] Refer also to Henri de Lubac's Christian Resistance to Anti-Semitism: Memories from 1940-1944; New York: The Miriam Press, 1990.

torture, and murder? Of course not. What it comes down to is realizing that sin is always possible. When we, as members of the Church, commit sin by going against the Church's teachings, this does not mean that the whole Church is evil. It simply means that individual members are failing in their efforts to follow the Lord as they should, and people suffer as a result. Christ, though, has, in revealing us to ourselves, called us to a higher standard in his own suffering and death, and "[a]t one and the same time . . . taught man to do good by his suffering and to do good to those who suffer. In this double aspect [Christ] has completely revealed the meaning of suffering" (*Salvifici doloris*, § 30).

Some words of Saint John Paul II about the Holocaust display this Catholic sense of the Cross in its universal application:

> The history of Europe is marked by discord not only in the sphere of states and politics. In conjunction with political interests and social — problems, these have resulted in bitter fighting, in the oppression and expulsion of dissenters, in repression and intolerance. As heirs to our forebears, we also place this guilt-ridden Europe under the Cross. For in the Cross is our hope. . . .
>
> Let us pray together (Catholics and Jews) that it (the Holocaust) will never happen again ... it makes us still more aware of the abyss which humanity can fall into when we do not acknowledge other people as brothers and sisters, sons and daughters, of the same heavenly father. It is the teaching of both the Hebrew and Christian Scriptures that the Jews are beloved of God, who has called them with an irrevocable calling. No valid theological justification could ever be found for acts of discrimination or

persecution against Jews. In fact, such acts must be held to be sinful.[72]

With all the explanations we can come up with as to why someone might think something that is absolutely wrong is justified, there still remains the fact that violence is always an appealing solution to those under pressure of their own uncontrolled emotions of fear or greed. No group or nation has a monopoly on evil or on good in terms of behavior of their people under stress. As Habakkuk implies, it is not God who is doing this to us, but we who are doing it to one another.

Does this mean that, since in every religion we can find a history of atrocities, we should not be part of any religious group? First of all, such a solution to the problem conceals the premise that I, by myself, am perfect and would not act wrongly under stress of any kind! In reality, most people are much better in terms of ethical actions when they are surrounded by groups who profess belief in God. Though each person falls short, communities that strive for more often achieve more.

What about when single or married persons sin in a sexual manner that is scandalous and injurious not only to the victims but also to themselves? When a priest, Sister, or Brother does so, it seems to strike Catholics and non-Catholics even more forcefully. To even imagine promising chastity is something so noble that failure to live up to it may seem even worse. Also there enters into the picture the problem of the victim often being a young person whose trust has been violated. Sad, distressing and agonizing as such sins are, are they reason to leave the Catholic Church or to stay away from her?

---

[72] John Paul II's On the Holocaust, edited by Eugene J. Fisher, Secretariat for Catholic- Jewish Relations, National Conference of Catholic Bishops, Washington, D.C., 1988.

Again, the failure to live up to an ideal is not a reason to throw out the ideal. When a Catholic prays the Apostles' Creed, he or she does not say, "I believe in Father X or Sister Y or Brother Z." Nor does someone enter into love relationships or marriage because he or she has only seen holy models of chastity and fidelity. Praying for God's grace, we should try to avoid all sin ourselves and we should also pray for and support anyone, whether the individual is a leader or not, who seems to be struggling with temptation or to have given in to it. How much sexual sin results from loneliness? — loneliness that could have been somewhat alleviated by our friendship!

Next, under the topic of evils of the Church, comes the question of luxury of Church art or of the clergy's lifestyle in the face of the needs of the poor. Over and over again in the history of the Church, reformers have asked: "Why not sell all the gold in Church art, sell grand buildings and give the money to the poor?" Jesus was poor, so why are his priests decked out in jeweled crowns, their standard of living higher than the people they minister to?

An analogy may help. Most North Americans of the United States feel proud to call themselves Americans in spite of our terrible history of negation of basic rights of Native Americans and African Americans. Why? Why not flee to another country with a better historical record? If pressed, most Americans would say that it is because we believe that our Constitution is good despite the fact that some Americans have violated its spirit in the past.

In a similar way, we can love a church that teaches love even if some of its members do what is unloving. The Catholic Church, in fact, does not claim that all her members are good and holy. Quite the opposite! We are told about our need for cleansing and purification. Even popes, bishops, priests and nuns are expected to seek sacramental reconciliation for their sins.

Within the Church we have the remedy for evil: the word of God and the sacraments. The millions of good Catholics throughout all times who have done God's will out of love for family and neighbor were living up to their faith. The ones who succumbed to evil were betraying it. Living our faith requires more than material observances, of course, more than an ontic understanding of the origins of pain. It requires awareness not only of the natural dimension, but also of the supernatural dimension that provides the form of the material world we inhabit. An awareness of suffering can be contextualized in no less a way.

We find within our suffering, then, its true meaning, which Saint John Paul II identified in *Salvifici doloris* as "truly supernatural and at the same time human. It is supernatural because it is rooted in the divine mystery of the Redemption of the world, and it is likewise deeply human, because in it the person discovers himself, his own humanity, his own dignity, his own mission" (§ 31). In the recognition of this, then, we resolve the paradox of the squared circle as we study the supernal face of God, yearning to know, just as Dante did in the last lines of his *Paradiso*, "just how our image merges into [God through the second Person of the Trinity], and how it there finds place" (Canto XXXIII, lines 138-139). The meaning of all human suffering is explained in the crucified Christ, and we find in that truth our own temporal healing and eternal salvation. The problem of pain is really a door into eternity.

Chapter 6: Morality and Atheism
by Ronda Chervin, Ph.D.

This chapter is devoted to refuting the belief of many atheists that there is no difference between the ethics of atheists and the ethics of theists. I believe there is a profound difference. Certainly, many atheists have some of the same moral ideals as theists do. There are atheists who are kind, helpful, honest and sacrificial. So, where do the differences come in? When I was an atheist in the 1950's there was one very profound difference between my ethics and those who were theists of any kind: Jewish, Christian or Islamic. This difference lies in the ethical skepticism/relativism of most atheists, which is necessarily opposed to the ethical universalism/absolutism of most theists.

Forms of Skepticism and Relativism

1. *Ethical Skepticism.* No human being is God, so you should not claim to know anything with absolute certainty, especially not concerning morality.

2. *Cultural Relativism.* There are different ideas of right and wrong in other cultures. One should not set up the norms of one's own society as an absolute. Since 500 miles away, the people might accept as natural the same act morally frowned upon in our country; therefore, we should realize that moral rules are arbitrary. George Bernard Shaw argued that morals are mostly only social habits and circumstantial necessities. A. J. Ayer claims that the causes of moral phenomena are psychological rather than ethical. Saying 'thou shalt' is but another way of registering your own desire that the other

perform in a certain manner; it has nothing to do with moral absolutes.

3. *Marxist Relativism*. We are all conditioned by economic and historical forces to set up certain values as absolutes, but there is no eternal sanction for any of them. This concept is especially important in Marxist philosophy, as indicated in the complicated but highly interesting quotation from Engels:

The conceptions of good and bad have varied so much from nation to nation and from age to age that they have often been in direct contradiction to each other. But all the same, someone may object, good is not bad and bad is not good: if good is confused with bad there is an end to all morality, and everyone can do and leave undone whatever he cares.

If it was such an easy business there would certainly be no dispute at all over good and bad; everyone would know what was good and what was bad. But how do things stand today? What morality is preached to us today?

There is first Christian-feudal morality, inherited from past centuries of faith; and this again has two main subdivisions, Catholic and Protestant moralities, each of which in turn has no lack of further subdivisions from the Jesuit-Catholic and Orthodox-Protestant to loose, 'advanced' moralities. Alongside of these we find the modern bourgeois morality and with it, too, the proletarian morality of the future, so that in the most advanced European countries alone the past, present and future provide three groups or moral theories which are in force simultaneously and alongside of each other. Which is then the true one? Not one of them, in the sense of having absolute validity.

But when we see that the three classes of modern society, the feudal aristocracy, the bourgeoisie and the proletariat, each have their special morality, we can only draw the one conclusion, that men, consciously or unconsciously, derive their moral ideas in the last resort from the practical relations on which they carry on production and exchange.

But nevertheless there is much that is common to the three moral theories mentioned above—is this not at least a portion of a morality which is externally fixed? These moral theories represent three different stages of the same historical development, and have therefore a common historical background, and for that reason alone they necessarily have much in common. Even more, in similar or approximately similar stages of economic development moral theories must of necessity be more or less in agreement.

From the moment when private property in movable objects developed, in all societies in which this private property existed there must be this moral law in common: Thou shalt not steal. Does this law thereby become an eternal moral law? By no means. In a society in which the motive for stealing has been done away with, in which therefore at the very most only lunatics would ever steal, how the teacher of morals would be laughed at who tried solemnly to proclaim the eternal truth: Thou shalt not steal!

We therefore reject every attempt to impose on us any moral dogma whatsoever as an eternal, ultimate and forever immutable moral law on the pretext that the moral world has its permanent principles which transcend history and the differences between nations. We maintain on the contrary that all former moral theories are the product, in the last analysis, of the economic stage which society had hitherto moved in class antagonisms, morality was always a class morality: it has either justified the domination and the interests of the ruling class, or, as soon as the oppressed class has become powerful enough, it has represented the revolt against this domination and the future interests of the oppressed.[73]

We must understand these theories in order to able to point their advocates to realism—real solutions to real problems. But we also must keep in mind that theories are developed to explain and solve problems that keep people from happiness. The danger of bad theory—or bad theoretical pieces—is that they chain us to a solution that perpetuate—and even worsens—the original problem.

Having presented in outline the three main standpoints favoring the idea that there are no absolutes — Ethical Skepticism, Cultural Relativism, and Marxist Relativism— let us now turn to some refutations:

1. Ethical Skepticism is the theory that we cannot know anything for certain. Even though we cannot know all truth because we are only finite human beings, it is still possible to have some valid insights—to understand part of the whole including recognizing the nature of reality. Look at this list of acts. Underline those you think are certainly wrong and put a question mark next to those you think could be right:

a) torture of an innocent human being
b) murder of an innocent human being
c) maiming a child
d) causing an innocent friend to go to jail for life
e) being a spy for an evil group of people who are enslaving one hundred innocent people
f) to rape someone
g) earning your living by setting up a slave system.

---

[73] Friedrich Engels, "The Communist Manifesto," from The Marx-Engels Reader, ed. Robert C. Tucker (New York: Wm. C. Norton & Co., Inc., 1978), p. 489.

Do you think that you would have to be God in order to be sure about the wrongness of those acts above?

Here is another relevant question: why is it that when we are the victim of a blatant injustice that we are perfectly sure that the act was wrong, whereas when we are strongly tempted to do something usually considered wrong, we are quick to invoke as an excuse the idea that there are no moral absolutes? For example, if a teacher gives an unfair grade you may not react by saying—'Maybe he (or she) is right. There are no moral absolutes.' But if you want to cheat you will most likely deny that cheating is totally wrong. Inconsistencies may point to flaws in your understanding that may lead us to an accurate understanding of reality.

2. Cultural Relativism is based on the fact that people in different cultures have varying moral rules. A plurality of rules does not prove, though, that no one rule is better than another. It can be argued, furthermore, that even if people of different cultures differ in the application of basic moral ideas to specific cases, most agree on the essence. C. S. Lewis refutes such relativism in *Mere Christianity* as follows:

> EVERYONE HAS HEARD people quarreling. Sometimes it sounds funny and sometimes it sounds merely unpleasant; but however it sounds, I believe we can learn something very important from listening to the kinds of things they say. They say things like this: "How'd you like it if anyone did the same to you?"--'That's my seat, I was there first"--"Leave him alone, he isn't doing you any harm"--"Why should you shove in first?"--"Give me a bit of your orange, I gave you a bit of mine"--"Come on, you promised." People say things like that every day, educated people as well as uneducated, and children as well as grown-ups.
>
> Now what interests me about all these remarks is that the man who makes them is not merely saying that the

other man's behavior does not happen to please him. He is appealing to some kind of standard of behavior which he expects the other man to know about. And the other man very seldom replies: "To hell with your standard." Nearly always he tries to make out that what he has been doing does not really go against the standard, or that if it does there is some special excuse. He pretends there is some special reason in this particular case why the person who took the seat first should not keep it, or that things were quite different when he was given the bit of orange, or that something has turned up which lets him off keeping his promise.

It looks, in fact, very much as if both parties had in mind some kind of Law or Rule of fair play or decent behavior or morality or whatever you like to call it, about which they really agreed. And they have. If they had not, they might, of course, fight like animals, but they could not quarrel in the human sense of the word. Quarreling means trying to show that the other man is in the wrong. And there would be no sense in trying to do that unless you and he had some sort of agreement as to what Right and Wrong are; just as there would be no sense in saying that a footballer had committed a foul unless there was some agreement about the rules of football.

Now this Law or Rule about Right and Wrong used to be called the Law of Nature. Nowadays, when we talk of the "laws of nature" we usually mean things like gravitation, or heredity, or the laws of chemistry. But when the older thinkers called the Law of Right and Wrong "the Law of Nature," they really meant the Law of Human Nature. The idea was that, just as all bodies are governed by the law of gravitation and organisms by biological laws, so the creature called man also had his law--with this great difference, that a body could not choose whether it obeyed the law of gravitation or not, but a man could choose either to obey the Law of Human Nature or to disobey it.

We may put this in another way. Each man is at every moment subjected to several sets of law but there is only one of these which he is free to disobey. As a body, he is subjected to gravitation and cannot disobey it; if you leave him unsupported in mid-air, he has no more choice about falling than a stone has. As an organism, he is subjected to various biological laws which he cannot disobey any more than an animal can. That is, he cannot disobey those laws which he shares with other things; but the law which is peculiar to his human nature, the law he does not share with animals or vegetables or inorganic things, is the one he can disobey if he chooses.

This law was called the Law of Nature because people thought that everyone knew it by nature and did not need to be taught it. They did not mean, of course, that you might not find an odd individual here and there who did not know it, just as you find a few people who are color-blind or have no ear for a tune. But taking the race as a whole, they thought that the human idea of decent behavior was obvious to everyone. And I believe they were right. If they were not, then all the things we said about the war were nonsense. What was the sense in saying the enemy was in the wrong unless Right is a real thing which the Nazis at bottom knew as well as we did and ought to have practiced! If they had no notion of what we mean by right, then, though we might still have had to fight them, we could no more have blamed them for that than for the color of their hair.

I know that some people say the idea of a Law of Nature or decent behavior known to all men is unsound, because different civilizations and different ages have had quite different moralities.

But this is not true. There have been differences between their moralities, but these have never amounted to anything like a total difference. If anyone will take the trouble to compare the moral teaching of, say, the ancient Egyptians, Babylonians, Hindus, Chinese, Greeks and Romans, what will really strike him will be how very like they are to each other and to our own. Some of the evidence for this I have put together in the appendix of another book called *The Abolition of Man*; but for our present purpose I need only ask the reader to think what a totally different morality would mean. Think of a country where people were admired for running away in battle, or where a man felt proud of double-crossing all the people who had been kindest to him. You might just as well try to imagine a country where two and two made five. Men have differed as regards what people you ought to be unselfish to--whether it was only your own family, or your fellow countrymen, or everyone. But they have always agreed that you ought not to put Yourself first. Selfishness has never been admired. Men have differed as to whether you should have one wife or four. But they have always agreed that you must not simply have any woman you liked.

But the most remarkable thing is this. Whenever you find a man who says he does not believe in a real Right and Wrong, you will find the same man going back on this a moment later. He may break his promise to you, but if you try breaking one to him he will be complaining "It's not fair" before you can say Jack Robinson. A nation may say treaties do not matter; but then, next minute, they spoil their case by saying that the particular treaty they want to break was an unfair one. But if treaties do not matter, and if there is no such thing as Right and Wrong--in other words, if there is no Law of Nature--what is the difference between a fair treaty and an unfair one? Have they not let the cat out of the bag and shown that, whatever they say, they really know the Law of Nature just like anyone else?

It seems, then, we are forced to believe in a real Right and Wrong People may be sometimes mistaken about them, just as people sometimes get their sums wrong; but they are not a matter of mere taste and opinion any more than the multiplication table. Now if we are agreed about that, I go on to my next point, which is this. None of us are really keeping the Law of Nature. If there are any exceptions among you, 1 apologize to them. They had much better read some other work, for nothing I am going to say concerns them. And now, turning to the ordinary human beings who are left:

I hope you will not misunderstand what I am going to say. I am not preaching, and Heaven knows I do not pretend to be better than anyone else. I am only trying to call attention to a fact; the fact that this year, or this month, or, more likely, this very day, we have failed to practice ourselves the kind of behavior we expect from other people. There may be all sorts of excuses for us. That time you were so unfair to the children was when you were very tired. That slightly shady business about the money--the one you have almost forgotten-came when you were very hard up. And what you promised to do for old So-and-so and have never done--well, you never would have promised if you had known how frightfully busy you were going to be. And as for your behavior to your wife (or husband) or sister (or brother) if I knew how irritating they could be, I would not wonder at it--and who the dickens am I, anyway? I am just the same. That is to say, I do not succeed in keeping the Law of Nature very well, and the moment anyone tells me I am not keeping it, there starts up in my mind a string of excuses as long as your arm. The question at the moment is not whether they are good excuses. The point is that they are one more proof of how deeply, whether we like it or not, we believe in the Law of Nature. If we do not believe in decent behavior, why should we be so anxious to make excuses for not having behaved decently? The truth is, we believe in decency so much--we feel the Rule of Law pressing on us so--that we cannot bear to face the fact that we are breaking it, and consequently we try to shift the responsibility. For you notice that it is only for our bad behavior that we find all these explanations. It is only our bad temper that we put down to being tired or worried or hungry; we put our good temper down to ourselves.

These, then, are the two points I wanted to make. First, that human beings, all over the earth, have this curious idea that they ought to behave in a certain way, and cannot really get rid of it. Secondly, that they do not in fact behave in that way. They know the Law of Nature; they break it. These two facts are the foundation of all clear thinking about ourselves and the universe we live in.[74]

Test what Lewis says by observing if what he says is true in yourself and those around you. Dietrich Von Hildebrand also refutes relativism as follows:

The first well-known argument for ethical relativism appeals to the diversity of moral judgments which can be found in different peoples, cultural realms, and historical epochs. What is considered as morally good or morally evil, this view contends, differs according to peoples and historical ages. A Mohammedan considers polygamy morally justifiable. It does not occur to him to have any pangs of conscience in this respect. With an entirely good conscience he has different wives simultaneously. To a Christian this would seem immoral and impure. Of such

---

[74] C. S. Lewis, *Mere Christianity* (New York: The Macmillan Co., 1943), pp. 17-18.

diversity in judgments on what is morally good and what is evil, innumerable examples can be offered. Moreover this diversity of opinion concerning the moral color of something is to be found not only in comparing different peoples and epochs, but also in looking at the same epoch and even at the same individual at different times of his life.

Now this first argument for the relativity of moral values is based on an invalid syllogism. From the diversity of many moral judgments; from the fact that certain people hold a thing to be morally evil while other people believe the same thing to be morally correct, it is inferred that moral values are relative, that there exists no moral good and evil, and that the entire moral question is tantamount to a superstition or a mere illusion.

In truth, a difference of opinion in no way proves that the object to which the opinion refers does not exist; or that it is in reality a mere semblance, changing for each individual or at least for different peoples. The fact that the Ptolemaic system was for centuries considered correct but is now superseded by our present scientific opinion is no justification for denying that the stars exist or even that our present opinion has only a relative validity.

There exist a great many fields in which can be found a diversity of opinion, among different peoples and in different epochs, and also among philosophers. Does this then confute the existence of objective truth? Not at all. The truth of a proposition does not depend upon how many people agree to it, but solely upon whether or not it is in conformity with reality.

Even if all men shared a certain opinion, it could still be wrong, and the fact that very few grasp a truth does not therefore alter or lessen its objective validity. Even the evidence of a truth is not equivalent to the fact that every man grasps and accepts it immediately. In like manner, it is erroneous to conclude that there exists no objective moral norm, that moral good and evil are in reality illusions or fictions or that at least their pretention to objective validity is an illusion, only because we find many different opinions concerning what is considered to be morally good and evil.

What matters is to see that in all these diversities the notion of an objective value, of a moral good and evil, is always presupposed, even if there exist contradictory positions concerning the moral goodness of a certain attitude or action. And just as the meaning of objective truth is not touched by the fact that two persons hold opposite positions and each one claims his proposition to be true, so too the notion of moral good and evil, of something objectively valid which calls for obedience and appeals to our conscience, is always untouched, even if one man says that polygamy is evil and another that polygamy is morally permissible.

The distinction between something merely subjectively satisfying and advantageous for an egotistic interest on the one hand, and the morally good on the other hand, is always in some way implied.

Thus conflicting opinions concerning the moral illicitness of something, instead of dethroning the general notions of moral good and moral evil, clearly attest their objectivity. As the diversity of opinions reveals that objective truth as such is always presupposed and is consequently beyond all possibility of the collapse to which the truth of a single fact may be exposed, so the indispensable presupposition of an objective moral norm reveals itself majestically in all diversities of opinions concerning the moral goodness or badness of a single attitude.

On the other hand, the fact that there have existed many more conflicting opinions concerning moral values, for instance, the moral character of polygamy or of blood revenge, than concerning colors or the size of corporeal things, can easily be understood as soon as we realize the moral requirements for a sound and integral value perception.

Without any doubt the perception of moral values differs in many respects from knowledge in any other field. In order to grasp the real value or disvalue of an attitude, in order to see, for example, the disvalue of revenge or polygamy, (more moral presuppositions are required than for any other type of knowledge. Reverence, a sincere thirst for truth, intellectual patience, and a spiritual *souplesse* are required in varying degrees for every adequate knowledge of any kind. But in the case of the moral value-perception much more is required: not only another degree of reverence and of opening our mind to the voice of being, a higher degree of "conspiring" with the object, but also a readiness of our will to conform to the call of values, whatever it may be. The influence of the environment, of the milieu, of the traditions of a community, in short the entire interpersonal atmosphere in which man grows up and lives, has a much greater influence on this type of knowledge than on any other. In the ethos of a community, moral convictions are present in another way than are convictions concerning other spheres. They are embodied not only in the laws and customs, but above all in the common ideal which forms an ever-present pattern for judging our fellow men and ourselves. The entire atmosphere is so saturated with this moral pattern that the conscious and unconscious influence on the individual is a tremendous one. . . .

Sometimes we find that those who are in a rage against the notion of any objective norm and any objective value nevertheless strive against them in the name of 'freedom' or 'democracy'; and thereby they fully admit the character of the value of freedom or democracy. They do not speak of freedom as if it were something merely agreeable or as if they wanted it for personal reasons, but they speak of it as an 'ideal.'[75]

What is required of us—in order to understand the natural law—is an openness to reality. For when we are open, we attune our sensitivity to the patterns give people seeking direction an understanding of the road to goodness and joy.

3. Marxist Relativism is based on the theory that morality reflects the economic conditions of a people rather than an absolute ethical stance. Although theoreticians such as Engels claim that morality is no more than an effect of economic conditions, it is impossible for them to actually hold this concept consistently. Why? Communist ideology involves inspiring people in non-Communist countries to revolt in indignation against the moral evils of capitalism. We are supposed to detest the injustice of exploitation of the poor.

But how could we truly believe exploitation to be unjust if there is no such thing as justice, if justice is merely a bourgeois concept caused by economic necessity? What is more, we are supposed to be motivated by our moral indignation to actually sacrifice our lives and those of others for the victory of the Party. To sacrifice for the future of the human race presupposes that it is good to altruistically set aside our own legitimate personal desires for the good of others. How can altruism be a virtue if there are no virtues, only economic conditions favoring a false belief that virtues are ethically good?

---

[75] Dietrich Von Hildebrand, *Ethics* (Chicago: Franciscan Herald Press, 1953), pp. 108ff.

Catholic Moral Teachings: Right or Wrong

An atheist might have read the above section of this chapter and agree that there are some universal moral truths but still have many disagreements about their application to specific controversial issues. The use of philosophical arguments along with Scripture and Tradition can demonstrate the truth of these moral concepts held by many theists.

Social Justice[76]

Central Problem: Minimalism—the idea that Christians can pursue their own individual needs with a minimum of concern for others.

Scripture and Tradition: "Is not this the fast that I choose: to loose the bonds of injustice, to undo the thongs of the yoke, to let the oppressed go free, to break every yoke? Is it not to share your bread with the hungry?" (Isaiah 58:6-7).

This teaching has been confirmed many times in encyclicals about social justice by Saint John Paul II. Each individual Catholic can exercise his or her conscience to determine how to apply such norms to specific responsibilities in the community.

Ethics of War

Central Problem: Because of nationalism and other causes, many Christians fail to see that most wars are unjust and therefore anti-Christian. We should not automatically support any war our country decides to engage in.

---

[76] Ronda Chervin, *Living in Love: About Christian Ethics* (Boston: St. Paul Books and Media), 2006. Online July 1, 2013, at http://www.rondachervin.com/pages/pdf/LivinginLove.pdf.

Scripture and Tradition: Proclamations about peace are innumerable in the Bible and in Catholic teaching. Jesus continually greets others with the words "Peace be to you." He proclaims that the peacemakers shall be blessed (Matthew 5:9), and He is called the Prince of Peace. On the other hand, the role of being a soldier was not looked down upon, in itself, as evil even though it certainly includes the possibility of killing (see Luke 3.10-14).

In the 1973 U.S. bishops' pastoral letter "The Challenge of Peace," there is a summary of our long tradition of condemning deliberate killing of the innocent. An update, "The Harvest of Justice Is Sown in Peace" (1993), stresses how, now that the threat of nuclear war has diminished, there is special need to underline the traditional teaching that war must be the last resort, not the first; how we must try to eliminate causes of violence and apply sanctions before killing people. Our tradition also insists that self-defense can be justified under certain conditions.

Here are some of the main points of the tradition called the just-war ethic from the Catechism of the Catholic Church:

2302 By recalling the commandment, "You shall not kill," [Mt. 5:21] our Lord asked for peace of heart and denounced murderous anger and hatred as immoral. Anger is a desire for revenge. "To desire vengeance in order to do evil to someone who should be punished is illicit," but it is praiseworthy to impose restitution "to correct vices and maintain justice." [St. Thomas Aquinas, ST II-II q158, a1 ad3] If anger reaches the point of a deliberate desire to kill or seriously wound a neighbor, it is gravely against charity; it is a mortal sin. The Lord says, "Everyone who is angry with his brother shall be liable to judgment." [Mt. 5:22]

2303 Deliberate hatred is contrary to charity. Hatred of the neighbor is a sin when one deliberately wishes him evil.

Hatred of the neighbor is a grave sin when one deliberately desires him grave harm. "But I say to you, Love your enemies and pray for those who persecute you, so that you may be sons of your Father who is in heaven." [Mt. 5:44-45]

2304 Respect for and development of human life require peace. Peace is not merely the absence of war, and it is not limited to maintaining a balance of powers between adversaries. Peace cannot be attained on earth without safeguarding the goods of persons, free communication among men, respect for the dignity of persons and peoples, and the assiduous practice of fraternity. Peace is "the tranquility of order." [St. Augustine, City of God 19, 13,1] Peace is the work of justice and the effect of charity. [Cf. Is. 32:17; cf. Vatican II, *Gaudium et spes* #78, 1-2]

2305 Earthly peace is the image and fruit of the peace of Christ, the messianic "Prince of Peace." [Is. 9:5] By the blood of his Cross, "in his own person he killed the hostility," [Eph. 2:16; cf. Col. 1:20-22] he reconciled men with God and made his Church the sacrament of the unity of the human race and of its union with God. "He is our peace." [Eph. 2:14] He has declared: "Blessed are the peacemakers." [Mt. 5:9]

2306 Those who renounce violence and bloodshed and, in order to safeguard human rights, make use of those means of defense available to the weakest, bear witness to evangelical charity, provided they do so without harming the rights and obligations of other men and societies. They bear legitimate witness to the gravity of the physical and moral risks of recourse to violence, with all its destruction and death. [Cf. Vatican II, *Gaudium et spes* 78, 5]

Avoiding war

2307 The fifth commandment forbids the intentional destruction of human life. Because of the evils and injustices that accompany all war, the Church insistently urges everyone to prayer and to action so that the divine Goodness may free us from the ancient bondage of war. [Cf. Vatican II, *Gaudium et spes* 81, 4] All citizens and all governments are obliged to work for the avoidance of war. However, "as long as the danger of war persists and there is no international authority with the necessary competence and power, governments cannot be denied the right of lawful self-defense, once all peace efforts have failed." [Cf. Vatican II, *Gaudium et spes* 79, 4]

2309 The strict conditions for legitimate defense by military force require rigorous consideration. The gravity of such a decision makes it subject to rigorous conditions of moral legitimacy. At one and the same time:
-    the damage inflicted by the aggressor on the nation or community of nations must be lasting, grave, and certain;
-    all other means of putting an end to it must have been shown to be impractical or ineffective;
-    there must be serious prospects of success;
-    the use of arms must not produce evils and disorders graver than the evil to be eliminated. The power of modern means of destruction weighs very heavily in evaluating this condition.

These are the traditional elements enumerated in what is called the "just war" doctrine. The evaluation of these conditions for moral legitimacy belongs to the prudential judgment of those who have responsibility for the common good.

2310 Public authorities, in this case, have the right and duty to impose on citizens the obligations necessary for national defense. Those who are sworn to serve their country in the armed forces are servants of the security and freedom of nations. If they carry out their duty honorably, they truly contribute to the common good of the nation and the maintenance of peace.[Cf. Vatican II, *Gaudium et spes* 79, 5]

2311 Public authorities should make equitable provision for those who for reasons of conscience refuse to bear arms; these are nonetheless obliged to serve the human community in some other way. [Cf. Vatican II, *Gaudium et spes* 79, 3] 2312 The Church and human reason both assert the permanent validity of the moral law during armed conflict. "The mere fact that war has regrettably broken out does not mean that everything becomes licit between the warring parties." [Cf. Vatican II, *Gaudium et spes* 79, 4]

2313 Non-combatants, wounded soldiers, and prisoners must be respected and treated humanely. Actions deliberately contrary to the law of nations and to its universal principles are crimes, as are the orders that command such actions. Blind obedience does not suffice to excuse those who carry them out. Thus the extermination of a people, nation, or ethnic minority must be condemned as a mortal sin. One is morally bound to resist orders that command genocide.

2314 "Every act of war directed to the indiscriminate destruction of whole cities or vast areas with their inhabitants is a crime against God and man, which merits firm and unequivocal condemnation." [Cf. Vatican II, *Gaudium et spes* 80, 3] A danger of modern warfare is that it provides the opportunity to those who possess modern scientific weapons—- especially atomic, biological, or chemical weapons—to commit such crimes.

2315 The accumulation of arms strikes many as a paradoxically suitable way of deterring potential adversaries from war. They see it as the most effective means of ensuring peace among nations. This method of deterrence gives rise to strong moral reservations. The arms race does not ensure peace. Far from eliminating the causes of war, it risks aggravating them. Spending enormous sums to produce ever new types of weapons impedes efforts to aid needy populations; [Pope Paul VI, *Populorum Progressio* 53] it thwarts the development of peoples. Over—armament multiplies reasons for conflict and increases the danger of escalation.

2316 The production and the sale of arms affect the common good of nations and of the international community. Hence public authorities have the right and duty to regulate them. The short-term pursuit of private or collective interests cannot legitimate undertakings that promote violence and conflict among nations and compromise the international juridical order.

2317 Injustice, excessive economic or social inequalities, envy, distrust, and pride raging among men and nations constantly threaten peace and cause wars. Everything done to overcome these disorders contributes to building up peace and avoiding war: Insofar as men are sinners, the threat of war hangs over them and will so continue until Christ comes again; but insofar as they can vanquish sin by coming together in charity, violence itself will be vanquished and these words will be fulfilled: "they shall beat their swords into plowshares, and their spears into pruning hooks; nation shall not lift up sword against nation, neither shall they learn war any more." [Cf. Vatican II, *Gaudium et spes* 78, 6; cf. Is. 2:4]

Abortion

Central Problem: Although everyone realizes that abortion is tragic, some think it could be the lesser of two evils in cases of mothers who are too young, too poor, unmarried, or incapable of dealing with a handicapped child or with rape or incest.

Scripture and Tradition. Exodus 23:7 tells us,"... do not kill the innocent and those in the right."

"Behold, children are a precious gift of the Lord, the fruit of the womb is a reward" (paraphrase of Psalm 127:3).

Psalm 139:13-16 describes the awesomeness surrounding conception: "For it was you who formed my inward parts; you knit me together in my mother's womb. . . . My frame was not hidden from you, when I was being made in secret, intricately woven in the depths of the earth. Your eyes beheld my unformed substance. In your book were written all the days that were formed for me, when none of them as yet existed."

The Documents of Vatican II warn us: " whatever is opposed to life itself, such as any type of murder, genocide, abortion, euthanasia, or willful self-destruction, whatever violates the integrity of the human person . . . all these things and others of their like are infamies indeed. They poison human society, but they do more harm to those who practice them than those who suffer from the injury. Moreover, they are a supreme dishonor to the Creator" (*Gaudium et spes*, "Pastoral Constitution on the Church in the Modern World," No. 27).

Compassion and real help for the mother pregnant against her own wishes should be extended generously as well as forgiveness for those who live in great pain repenting an abortion. Such loving attitudes and acts do not invalidate showing love to the baby through adoption, and through efforts to stop abortion by legal means and by nonviolent protest. Catholic Realism understands that the embryo is a person.

Euthanasia

Central Problem: Many people wonder whether the sustaining of life by extraordinary means even in cases involving great suffering or expense is required. In the case of someone in excruciating pain or born with extreme defects, could not a positive act of ending the life of such a person be more charitable than letting that individual live on?

Scripture and Tradition: "Thou shalt not kill" (see, for example, Exodus 20:13 and Luke 18:20). The biblical injunction against killing is supported by the very progressive Greek Hippocratic oath taken by all doctors, "I will neither give a deadly drug to anybody who asks for it, nor will I make a suggestion to this effect."

Direct killing of innocent persons for any reason has always been ruled out in Judeo-Christian morality. (In the case of war it is usually maintained that a person who unjustly kills others forfeits his or her right to life and is certainly not innocent.) Killing an innocent, including oneself, is a way of usurping God's power over creation and death. This doctrine was reiterated by Pope Pius XII during the Nazi times in response to questions of eugenics and genocide.

This doctrine also reflects the religious conviction that every human being is infinitely precious regardless of any consideration of development. We are creatures who owe our existence to God. We belong to him and we must accept the problems of suffering in our lives that remain even when we try to alleviate them by every pain-killing means available.

On the other hand, the Church teaches that we do not have to use extraordinary means to keep a person alive who is in great pain or causing tremendous burdens. What are extraordinary and what are ordinary means vary from age to age and culture to culture. This makes it difficult to apply some neat, exact measure. However, moral theologians normally say that ordinary means are those commonly accepted, readily available, without extreme difficulty in terms of pain and expense. Heroic measures that offer no reasonable hope of benefit do not have to be used; however, food and water are considered to be not medicine but an ordinary means to keep someone alive even if administered by a feeding tube that does not cause pain.

Divorce

Central Problem: As divorce and remarriage has become more and more acceptable in the society around us, many Christians question whether in some cases it might not be the most loving thing to humbly accept the fact that some marriages cause more pain than joy and some couples seem to be unable to be reconciled with each other. In such cases should not each be free to try to make a better life with someone else? Especially, should the innocent party who has been deserted or maltreated have to live singly for the rest of his or her life?

Scripture and Tradition: "It was also said, 'Whoever divorces his wife must give her a bill of divorce.' But I say to you, whoever divorces his wife (unless the marriage is unlawful)[77] causes her to commit adultery, and whoever

---

[77] The New American Bible explains "unlawful" as follows: "It seems . . . that the unlawfulness that Matthew gives as a reason why a marriage must be broken refers to a situation peculiar to his community: the violation of Mosaic law forbidding marriage between persons of certain blood and/or legal relationship (Lev 18:6-18).

marries a divorced woman commits adultery." (Matthew 5:31-32, NAB)

Further, in the gospel of Matthew (19:3-9) we are told: "Some Pharisees approached him, and tested him, saying, "Is it lawful for a man to divorce his wife for any cause whatever?" He said in reply, "Have you not read that from the beginning the Creator 'made them male and female' and said, 'For this reason a man shall leave his father and mother and be joined to his wife, and the two shall become one flesh'? So they are no longer two, but one flesh. Therefore, what God has joined together, no human being must separate." They said to him, "Then why did Moses command that the man give the woman a bill of divorce and dismiss (her)?" He said to them, "Because of the hardness of your hearts Moses allowed you to divorce your wives, but from the beginning it was not so. I say to you, whoever divorces his wife (unless the marriage is unlawful) and marries another commits adultery." (NAB)

The emphasis in Catholic tradition is on the importance of fidelity to the valid bond of love undertaken in marriage. Marriages can only be annulled if such a valid bond can be proven never to have existed, as in the case of those forced to marry, those who do not consummate their marriages in sexual intercourse due to sexual impotence, or, in recent times, those who purposely and consciously exclude the notion of marriage as a bond "till death do us part."

Of late, due to a greater knowledge of the effect of certain mental disorders on the freedom of the person, more marriages are being annulled on the basis of extreme

---

Marriages of that sort were regarded as incest (*porneia*), but some rabbis allowed Gentile converts to Judaism who had contracted such marriages to remain in them. Matthew's "exceptive clause" is against such permissiveness for Gentile converts to Christianity; cf the similar prohibition of porneia in Acts 15:20, 29. In this interpretation, the clause constitutes no exception to the absolute prohibition of divorce when the marriage is lawful."

213 | C a t h o l i c   R e a l i s m :   a   F r a m e w o r k   f o r   t h e
R e f u t a t i o n   o f   A t h e i s m   a n d   t h e   E v a n g e l i z a t i o n
o f   A t h e i s t s

immaturity making a free-will decision of self-donation impossible.[78]

A very beautiful summary of Church teaching on divorce is included in the U.S. bishops' pastoral letter of 1976 "To Live in Christ Jesus," from which I now quote:

> Every human being has a need and right to be loved, to have a home where he or she can put down roots and grow. The family is the first and indispensable community in which this need is met. Today, when productivity, prestige or even physical attractiveness are regarded as the gauge of personal worth, the family has a special vocation to be a place where people are loved not for what they do or what they have but simply because they are.
>
> A family begins when a man and woman publicly proclaim before the community their mutual commitment so that it is possible to speak of them as one body. Christ teaches that God wills the union of man and woman in marriage to be life long, a sharing of life for the length of life itself.
>
> The Old Testament takes the love between husband and wife as one of the most powerful symbols of God's love for His people: "I will espouse you to Me forever: I will espouse you in right and in justice, in love and in mercy: I will espouse you in fidelity, and you shall know the Lord." So

---

[78] This overuse of "lack of discretion of judgment" has been challenged significantly by now-Cardinal Raymond Burke, who explains, rather poignantly, that "[w]hen a lack of discretion of judgment no longer has its cause in some pathology, then every 'unhappiness' in marriage suddenly becomes a sign of nullity of consent" and posits that "the 'unhappiness' may be quite simply the invitation to live more intensely 'conjugal charity,' to find true happiness in the acceptance of suffering for love's sake" (208). See Raymond Burke, "Lack of Discretion of Judgment: Canonical Doctrine and Legislation," *The Jurist* 45 (1985): 171-209.

husband and wife espouse themselves, joined in a holy and loving covenant.

The New Testament continues this imagery: only now the union between husband and wife rises to the likeness of the union between Christ and His Church. Jesus teaches that in marriage men and women are to pledge steadfast unconditional faithfulness which mirrors the faithfulness of the Son of God. Their marriages make this fidelity and love visible to the world. Christ raised marriage in the Lord to the level of a sacrament, whereby this union symbolizes and affects God's special love for the couple in their total domestic and social situation.

Jesus tells us that the Father can and will grant people the greatness of heart to keep such pledges of loving faithfulness. The Church has always believed that in making and keeping noble promises of this sort people can, through the grace of God, grow beyond themselves — grow to the point of being able to love beyond their merely human capacity. Yet contemporary culture makes it difficult for many people to accept this view of marriage. Even some who admire it as an ideal doubt whether it is possible and consider it too risky to attempt. They believe it is better to promise less at the start and so be able to escape from marital tragedy in order to promise once again.

But this outlook itself has increased marital tragedy. Only men and women bold enough to make promises for life, believing that with God's help they can be true to their word as He is to His, have the love and strength to surmount the inevitable challenges of marriage. Such unselfish love, rooted in faith, is ready to forgive when the need arises and to make the sacrifices demanded if something as precious and holy as marriage is to be preserved. For the family to be a place where human beings can grow with security, the love pledged by husband and wife must have as its model the selfless and enduring love of Christ for the Church. "Husbands, love your wives, as Christ loved the Church. He gave himself up for her."

Some say even valid sacramental marriages can deteriorate to such an extent that the marital union dies and the spouses are no longer obliged to keep their promise of lifelong fidelity. Some even urge the Church to acknowledge such dissolution and allow the parties to enter new, more promising unions. We reject this view. In reality it amounts to a proposal to forego Christian marriage at the outset and substitute something entirely different. It would weaken marriage further, by paying too little heed to Jesus' call to identify ourselves with His redeeming love, which endures all things. Its fundamental difficulty is that it cannot be reconciled with the Church's mission to be faithful to the word entrusted to it. The covenant between a man and woman joined in Christian marriage is as indissoluble and irrevocable as God's love for His people and Christ's love for His Church.

We must seek ways by which the Church can mediate Christ's compassion to those who have suffered marital tragedy, but at the same time we may do nothing to undermine His teaching concerning the beauty and meaning of marriage and in particular His prophetic demands concerning the indissolubility of the unions of those who marry in the Lord. The Church must ever be faithful to the command to serve the truth in love.

The practice of some couples in second marriages to receive Communion without an annulment is not allowable except with permission in some cases where evidence of the nullity of the previous marriages is unobtainable as, for instance, in the case of documents destroyed in wartime. The life-long bond of marriage reflects the value and dignity of the persons. The bond cannot be broken because the dignity of the person can never be undone.

Premarital and Extramarital Sex

Central Problem: Given the tremendous emphasis on pleasure in contemporary society, it is very difficult for people to impose restraints on themselves. Also, since many think that marriages should not be entered into before the age of twenty-one or even later, it is thought to be too difficult to restrain sexual needs until that time. Although most Christians reject free love, some think that in the case of an engaged couple who have to wait a long time for marriage, premarital intercourse could be permitted. Others think that in the case of marriages involving great difficulties, extramarital sex might be licit.

Scripture and Tradition: The scriptural word for premarital sex is "fornication," and for extramarital sex "adultery." Some claim that these matters are not emphasized in Scripture because they do not realize what these terms refer to. There are many references in Scripture to the forbidding of any form of fornication or adultery — see especially the commandment "Neither shall you covet your neighbor's wife" (Deuteronomy 5:21); refer also, for example, to Matthew 5:27-30, Hebrews 13:4, and 1 Corinthians 6:9, 18.

Tradition has been very strong on these two temptations. Contrary to some opinions, these teachings have in no way been changed in recent years. They are reaffirmed in authoritative documents to the present.

Using another person for sexual pleasure alone violates that individual's dignity. Those who engage in recreational sex are value-blind to the deep meaning of this sphere, destined as it is to express the total self-donation of marriage and to be open to the procreation of a new human person — the baby.

But what if the motive is not lust but real love? Real love seeks commitment, not an open-ended affair. Great intimacy without the marriage bond leads to the devastating wound of rejection and also the tragic desire to get rid of any children whose conception occurs due to ineffective contraception.

Church history is full of examples of happy, holy, chaste people who did not think having sexual intimacy was a necessity, beginning with Mary, Joseph and Jesus.

Contraception

Central Problem: Due to the great difficulty of raising families in cities, the problem of poverty and many other obstacles, many couples think it unwise to have large families.

Of these, many are unacquainted with the natural rhythms of the woman's fertile cycle, which when properly understood requires only a minimum of abstinence from sexual intercourse to avoid an untimely pregnancy. This state of affairs has made artificial contraception more and more attractive as an alternative for many Christian couples.

Scripture and Tradition: Throughout history many different methods of preventing birth have been used, including the use of drugs and magic, or sorcery (see, for instance, Galatians 5:20 and Revelation 21:8, 22:15). Throughout history the Church has condemned such practices over and over again, culminating in Pope Paul VI's encyclical *Humanae Vitae*, which was promulgated on July 25, 1968. Since then, attention has also been paid to the added grave immorality of pills, IUD's (intrauterine devices) and the like that really abort the already fertilized egg. It is Catholic teaching that human life begins at conception. Not too long ago all Christian churches agreed with the Catholic position on contraceptives. It was understood that fertility was a gift of God, even if a burden, just as is all of life on earth.

In Catholic teaching through the centuries the emphasis has been on our call to use the gifts God has given us in ways that do not violate their God-given nature. I should use my voice to tell truth, not abuse its communicative nature by telling lies. I should use my reproductive organs in a life-giving way, not abuse them by sterilization, by intentionally blocking conception or by distorting a woman's entire system with contraceptive pills. One can think of the fertile time of a woman's cycle as a sacred time. A woman should be proud that she has this gift rather than violating that time. Natural Family Planning sets the gift aside by not using it, whereas contraceptives use that time while abusing it.

Does that mean couples should have one baby after another no matter what their circumstances? No. Not any more than a person need talk incessantly. We can remain silent when speech would be hurtful — as do those who refuse to reveal the whereabouts of persons searched for by criminals or by tyrants who intend to kill them. In a similar way we can decide not to use the fertile time in a woman's cycle — only a few days — during times when serious reasons make it better to postpone the coming of a new baby. The new methods of Natural Family Planning are easy, and when used appropriately have a much higher rate of effectiveness than most unnatural methods.

Many Catholic theologians who originally dissented from magisterial teaching on this subject have come to see how dreadful are the effects of the contraceptive culture on young people as well as on married ones. It is clear that the use of contraceptives gives people a false sense of security in pursuing sex outside of marriage and adulterous sex. A contraceptive failure often leads to the aborting of the child.[79]

---

[79] For more information on this subject see Dr. Janet Smith's "Contraception: Why Not" series at http://www.janetesmith.org. Dr. Smith points out that "that couples using natural family planning almost never divorce" (p. 24, http://www.janetesmith.org/documents/OfficialTranscriptContracept ionWhyNot.pdf).

Homosexuality

Central Problem: In recent years, due to psychological, sociological and moral causes there has been an enormous increase in open homosexuality. Agitation among homosexuals, many of whom consider themselves to be Christians, has led to the legalization of homosexual marriages in many states.

Scripture and Tradition: Scripture refers to homosexuality, masturbation, fornication with animals, etc., as unnatural and unclean acts. Passages can be found condemning them in Genesis 19:5 (note that in Scripture "to know" in a sexual context means intercourse); Leviticus 18 and 20:13; Judges 19:22; Wisdom 14:22-29; Ephesians 4:19. And the most oft-quoted-Romans 1:26-28, 32 - tells us: "For this reason God gave them up to degrading passions. Their women exchanged natural intercourse for unnatural, and in the same way also the men, giving up natural intercourse with women, were consumed with passion for one another. Men committed shameless acts with men and received in their own persons the due penalty for their error. And since they did not see fit to acknowledge God, God gave them up to a debased mind and to things that should not be done. . . . They know God's decree, that those who practice such things deserve to die [that is, a spiritual death] — yet they not only do them but even applaud others who practice them."

The wrongness of homosexual practices has been reaffirmed over and over again through the present day in the Catholic tradition. For a refutation of arguments given to justify it see John Harvey's *Same Sex Attraction: Catholic Teaching, Pastoral Practice*.[80] Having a homosexual

---

[80] *Same Sex Attraction: Catholic Teaching, Pastoral Practice* (2007). Available online at http://www.kofc.org/un/en/resources/cis/cis385.pdf. See also the Congregation for the Doctrine of the Faith's "The Letter to the Bishops

orientation as opposed to practice is not in itself blame-worthy since many times it is rooted in psychological disorders. Growth in Christian maturity makes it possible to control such desires, and intense counseling may lead to healing of psychological problems, especially if the person involved wants to change.

As Pope Paul VI states: "The Master, who speaks with great severity in this matter [of chastity] (Mt. 5:28), does not propose an impossible thing. We Christians, regenerated in baptism, though we are not freed from this kind of weakness, are given the grace to overcome it" ("To Live the Paschal Mystery," May 1971). Many are the men and women who once thought the Church's teachings on morality were too strict but who later went on to embrace them, finally viewing them not as a prison but as liberation. Some famous ones are: Augustine, St. Ignatius Loyola, St. Francis of Assisi, Blessed Angela of Foligno, St. Margaret of Cortona, Charles de Foucauld, Malcolm Muggeridge, and Dorothy Day.

Changing Teachings within the Church?

Because so many dissented on the Church's prohibition of contraception, including the council that Pope Paul VI convened to study the issue of chemical contraceptives, it was claimed that since the Church has changed on other moral issues like usury and slavery, why not contraception?

In my book *Living in Love: About Christian Ethics*, I explained that there is such a thing as development of doctrine throughout history. The angelic salutation, "Mary, full of

---

of the Catholic Church on the Pastoral Care of Homosexual Persons" by then-Cardinal Joseph Ratzinger (1986; http://www.vatican.va/roman_curia/congregations/cfaith/document s/rc_con_cfaith_doc_19861001_homosexual-persons_en.html). For a psychologist's approach see Joseph Nicolosi's *Reparative Therapy for the Homosexual* (Northvale, N.J.: Jason Aronson, Inc., 1991).

grace," for instance, enabled us to understand as articles of faith both the Immaculate Conception (that Mary was conceived without the stain of original sin) and the Assumption (if she was full of grace she did not have to die). In the Old Testament, slavery was permitted and laws were promulgated about treating slaves well. In the New Testament, Paul entreats Philemon to treat Onesimus has his brother. In these and other ways, we see doctrine developing over time.

There is, furthermore, much to be found in Catholic teaching that would appear to allow for approaching moral decisions on an individual basis. In Vatican Council II we find these words: "It is through his conscience that man sees and recognizes the demands of the divine law. He is bound to follow this conscience faithfully in all his activity so that he may come to God, who is his last end. Therefore he must not be forced to act contrary to his conscience" ("Declaration on Religious Liberty," No. 3).

The council also explains: "Deep within his conscience man discovers a law which he has not laid upon himself but which he must obey. Its voice, ever calling him to love and do what is good and to avoid evil, tells him inwardly at the right moment: do this, shun that. For man has in his heart a law inscribed by God. His dignity lies in observing this law, and by it he will be judged. His conscience is man"s most secret core, and his sanctuary" ("Pastoral Constitution on the Church in the Modern World," No. 16).

Faced with hard choices in areas such as mercy killing, remarriage after divorce involving a valid marriage, contraception, homosexual activity, or engaging as a combatant in a war the justice of which is questionable, many people — whatever their philosophy or religion — will want to avoid fixed structures in favor of their own judgment of personal conscience.

Catholics caught in such dilemmas may consider "bending the rules" to "resolve" the dilemmas and make them acceptable on the basis of the apparent changes in Church teaching over the years on questions such as slavery, usury or the meaning of sex in marriage. Our noticing that even some Catholic theologians disagree about certain moral issues may also suggest the necessity of making up one's mind oneself. Behavior that seems contradictory to Scripture or tradition will often be debated by other Christians with questions such as: "The Bible condemns premarital sex as fornication, so how can you justify it?" or "How can you go to Holy Communion each week when you are living with someone to whom you are not married?" Such rebukes will sometimes receive a response such as this: "Jesus was merciful to sinners — where do you get off being so legalistic and self-righteous?"

And yet the whole idea of individual morality is contrary to a broader view of Scripture and tradition. Absolutizing personal conscience presupposes that all people are innocent and well-intended, eager to sacrifice their own individual needs in obedience to God for the good of others. While it is true that God made us to be good, very soon our first parents chose to disobey without concern for the consequences. After the fall of Adam and Eve, we all have a tendency to self-deception or what the moral philosopher Dietrich von Hildebrand called "value-blindness." Value-blindness is a form of self-deception. We know with what false reasoning slave traders rationalized their evil deeds. To justify their greed, slave traders convinced themselves that slaves were not real persons or that they were such children they could not live without masters. We find similar forms of value-blindness in our times whereby abortionists persuade themselves that a baby in the womb is not a real person.

In the Book of Proverbs (16:25) it is written, "Sometimes there is a way that seems to be right, but in the end it is the way to death." Dramatic examples of this kind of value-blindness undermining conscience to be found in Scripture are David's adultery with Bathsheba and his plot to kill her husband. In the New Testament, does not Caiaphas argue that the death of Jesus is justified for "the good of the people"? The status of the Jewish political leaders as friends of the Romans was not to be displaced by a Messiah-King.

A thoughtful reading of the Bible bears out the necessity of moral authority for less-than-perfect human creatures. As one speaker put it: it is not the ten suggestions; it is the Ten Commandments! Does that mean that there is no room for personal conscience? No. When we make choices between two good possibilities such as serving the community as a fire fighter or a doctor, we ought to decide on the basis of personal talents and circumstances.

However, Catholic tradition based on a scriptural understanding of human nature insists on the need for moral norms when it comes to the business of avoiding moral evils. In the Documents of Vatican II ("Pastoral Constitution on the Church in the Modern World"), this clarification is given: "when there is a question of harmonizing conjugal love with the responsible transmission of life, the moral aspect of any procedure does not depend solely on sincere intentions or on an evaluation of motives. It must be determined by objective standards" (No. 51). Respectful dissent from Church moral teaching is not even an accepted category for theologians, according to the "Instruction on the Ecclesial Vocation of the Theologian" [Origins, May 14, 1990, IV-B, Nos. 32-41).

Saint John Paul II's encyclical *Veritatis splendor* (or The Splendor of Truth), which came out in 1993, contains these words about how important it is that Christians not only be sincere but that they choose the good:

> The rational ordering of the human act to the good in its truth and the voluntary pursuit of that good, known by reason, constitute morality. Hence human activity cannot be judged as morally good merely because it is a means for attaining one or another of its goals, or simply because the

subject's intention is good. Activity is morally good when it attests to and expresses the voluntary ordering of the person to his ultimate end and the conformity of a concrete action with the human good as it is acknowledged in its truth by reason. If the object of the concrete action is not in harmony with the true good of the person, the choice of that action makes our will and ourselves morally evil, thus putting us in conflict with our ultimate end, the supreme good, God himself. (§ 72)

About false teaching, Saint John Paul II writes:

No damage must be done to the harmony between faith and life: the unity of the Church is damaged not only by Christians who reject or distort the truths of faith but also by those who disregard the moral obligations to which they are called by the Gospel (cf. 1 Cor. 5:9-13). The Apostles decisively rejected any separation between the commitment of the heart and the actions which express or prove it (cf. 1 Jn. 2:3-6). And ever since Apostolic times the Church's Pastors have unambiguously condemned the behavior of those who fostered division by their teaching or by their actions. (§ 26)

Does that mean that Saint John Paul II has no sympathy for how hard the moral struggle is for Christians of our times? Not at all. He explains his teaching on weakness and mercy:

Only in the mystery of Christ's Redemption do we discover the 'concrete' possibilities of man. It would be a very serious error to conclude . . . that the Church's teaching is essentially only an 'ideal' which must then be adapted, proportioned, graduated to the so- called concrete possibilities of man, according to a 'balancing of the goods

225 | C a t h o l i c   R e a l i s m :   a   F r a m e w o r k   f o r   t h e
R e f u t a t i o n   o f   A t h e i s m   a n d   t h e   E v a n g e l i z a t i o n
o f   A t h e i s t s

in question.' But what are the 'concrete possibilities of man? And of which man are we speaking? Of man dominated by lust or of man redeemed by Christ? This is what is at stake: the reality of Christ's redemption. Christ has redeemed us! This means that he has given us the possibility of realizing the entire truth of our being; he has set our freedom free from the domination of concupiscence. And if redeemed man still sins, this is not due to an imperfection of Christ's redemptive act, but to man's will not to avail himself of the grace which flows from that act. God's command is of course proportioned to man's capabilities; but to the capabilities of the man to whom the Holy Spirit has been given; of the man who, though he has fallen into sin, can always obtain pardon and enjoy the presence of the Holy Spirit (§ 103).

In this context, appropriate allowance is made both for God's mercy towards the sinner who converts and for the understanding of human weakness. Such understanding never means compromising and falsifying the standard of good and evil in order to adapt it to particular circumstances. It is quite human for the sinner to acknowledge his weakness and to ask mercy for his failings; what is unacceptable is the attitude of one who makes his own weakness the criterion of the truth about the good, so that he can feel self-justified, without even the need to have recourse to God and his mercy. An attitude of this sort corrupts the morality of society as a whole, since it encourages doubt about the objectivity of the moral law in general and a rejection of the absoluteness of moral prohibitions regarding specific human acts, and it ends up by confusing all judgments about values (§ 104).

But what about so-called changed moral teaching of the past? To respond to this question it is necessary to do some research concerning each moral issue.

Slavery was never considered a good thing by the Catholic Church. As in Scripture, it was tolerated as an alternative to the more cruel practice of killing those captured in war. Slave- trading in later times was condemned by the Church, and slavery was outlawed by the Spanish at the urging of the Church in 1530, three hundred thirty-three years before President Abraham Lincoln issued the Emancipation Proclamation. Does that mean no Catholics had slaves? Slave owning was tolerated on the basis of the benefits to a slave of being owned by a benevolent person rather than tortured by an evil one. For the slave on the block, this was deemed to be a better alternative, until liberation was a legal possibility.

Here is a contemporary example of toleration vs. approval:

In one particular biblical concordance, there are more than two hundred entries under "just" and "justice" and thousands of others explaining how important it is to care deeply about the needs of the suffering. Although many disobedient, selfish Catholics have chosen to cling to luxurious lifestyles rather than give generously to the needy or donate time to creating more just societal patterns and laws, Church teaching is clear as to principle: "God destined the earth and all it contains for all men and all peoples so that all created things would be shared fairly by all mankind under the guidance of justice tempered by charity" (Vatican Council II, "Pastoral Constitution on the Church in the Modern World," § 69).

In his encyclical "On the Development of Peoples," Pope Paul VI summarized and applied the constant teaching of the Church in this regard:

> If someone who has the riches of this world sees his brother in need and closes his heart to him, how does the love of God abide in him? (1 Jn. 3:17) It is well known how strong were the words used by the Fathers of the Church to describe the proper attitude of persons who possess anything toward persons in need. To quote St. Ambrose: 'You are not making a gift of your possessions to the poor person. You are handing over to him what is his. For what is given in common for the use of all, you have arrogated to yourself. The world is given to all, and not only to the rich.' That is, private property does not constitute for anyone an absolute unconditioned right. No one is justified in keeping for his exclusive use what he does not need, when others lack necessities. In a word, according to the traditional doctrine as found in the Fathers of the Church and the great theologians, the right to property must never be exercised to the detriment of the common good. (§23)

Usury, which is charging exorbitant interest in order to exploit others, remains condemned. In early times of the Church, the practice of giving loans was always exploitative. Later, legitimate banking practices proved that granting loans at small interest could be a benefit to the needy.

If in fact moral teachings in their essence have not changed, does this mean that every Catholic simply renounces his or her conscience and just asks the priest what to do in every aspect of life? Not really. Although obedience to legitimate authority, called by God to shepherd us, is always right and good, we are also called to ponder God's will in our hearts — to love his law. Jesus is merciful but also firm. "Your sins are forgiven . . . and from now on do not sin again" (Luke 7:48 and John 8:11).

Conclusion

If an atheist accepts any of the arguments presented in this chapter for the reality of moral absolutes, then he or she has to ask why a moral principle could be absolute in the first place. To be an absolute raises the moral principle to the status of a law, and all law requires a lawgiver. St. Thomas defines law in ST I-II, Q. 90, Art. 4 as "nothing else than an ordinance of reason for the common good, made by him who has care of the community, and promulgated."

The author of a civil law can be found in a human person, but the author of a moral law can only be traced through the natural law, which is, St. Thomas defines in ST I-II, Q. 91, Art. 2, "nothing else than the rational creature's participation of the eternal law," which St. Thomas defines in ST I-II, Q. 93, Art. 1, as "nothing else than the type of Divine Wisdom, as directing all actions and movements." Any moral absolute, then, points by definition through natural law to God.

Even if many atheists accept these values in their understanding of morality as relative, it is much harder for them to live such values out without their doing so as an act of love of God. Even they must recognize the dissonance between their theories and how they bear out in practice. But dissonance is just a painful state that calls us to into harmony.

Chapter 7: Conclusion—The Impact of Atheism

Today, it is quite fashionable to be an atheist, so much so that theists may legitimately be uncertain of the presence of other theists in any given public gathering. This is why it is important for us to speak the truth to all persons in every way that will enable them to hear us. In so doing, we become a beacon of truth around which others might rally, and in our spiritual leadership over any group of which we are a part, we will find supporters there with us ready to take their stand. We will also find atheists who have read the works of the New Atheists—Richard Dawkins, Daniel Dennett, Christopher Hitchens and Samuel Harris—and who may identify with them in one way or another. Our question is a proactive one: how do we evangelize them?

Throughout this book, we learned that atheism in general is not monolithic. Just as there are many varieties of faith, there are many varieties of non-faith, or non-belief. *Gaudium et spes* lists some varieties of non-faith that lie in lack of true belief, explaining that

> [t]he word atheism is applied to phenomena which are quite distinct from one another. For while God is expressly denied by some, others believe that man can assert absolutely nothing about Him. Still others use such a method to scrutinize the question of God as to make it seem devoid of meaning. Many, unduly transgressing the limits of the positive sciences, contend that everything can be explained by this kind of scientific reasoning alone, or by contrast, they altogether disallow that there is any absolute truth. Some laud man so extravagantly that their

faith in God lapses into a kind of anemia, though they seem more inclined to affirm man than to deny God. Again some form for themselves such a fallacious idea of God that when they repudiate this figment they are by no means rejecting the God of the Gospel. Some never get to the point of raising questions about God, since they seem to experience no religious stirrings nor do they see why they should trouble themselves about religion. Moreover, atheism results not rarely from a violent protest against the evil in this world, or from the absolute character with which certain human values are unduly invested, and which thereby already accords them the stature of God. Modern civilization itself often complicates the approach to God not for any essential reason but because it is so heavily engrossed in earthly affairs. (§ 19)

Not to be overlooked among the forms of modern atheism is that which anticipates the liberation of man especially through his economic and social emancipation. This form argues that by its nature religion thwarts this liberation by arousing man's hope for a deceptive future life, thereby diverting him from the constructing of the earthly city. Consequently when the proponents of this doctrine gain governmental power they vigorously fight against religion, and promote atheism by using, especially in the education of youth, those means of pressure which public power has at its disposal. (§ 20)

We must dialogue with the truth and for the truth. We must witness to dialogue being a means to the end of truth instead of a means to the end of power.

All of these ways and reasons for the failure of true belief are grounded either in the worldview that there is a God to whom we cannot relate or in the worldview that there is no God to whom to relate. These competing paradigms of atheistic thought, then, are simply manifestations of the worldview out of which it comes. It is rarer that a paradigm will bring about a worldview, in fact, than it is that a person will fall into a paradigm because of his or her worldview. If we can address "worldview" in our evangelization, we can reshape receptivity toward belief and from belief, faith. A faith-filled life understands that the natural world was formed by an intelligent mind known as God for a meaningful purpose, namely to call human persons created in the image and likeness of God into joyful communion with himself. A faith-filled life is one in which Mary's command to the servants is fully actualized in us: "Do whatever he tells you" (John 2:5). This is a life filled with trust in Jesus Christ. The life devoid of faith, on the other hand, perceives only the natural world, unformed by anything but chance and adaptation of life to its changing circumstances, without purpose or meaning.

Not to see purpose or meaning to the life we live is its own kind of punishment because it leads ultimately to sterility, which is the opposite of the fecundity for which we were made. Such sterility is rather poignantly illustrated by Dante Alighieri, who features in the seventh circle of hell the soul of Capaneus, one of the seven who stood against Thebes and who, like the other blasphemers, hurtled barbs at God and now lies supine on the sands as those barbs return to him in the form of burning flakes. Seeing himself observed, Capaneus cries out, "Such as I was living, am I, dead" (Canto XIV, line 51). Upon hearing the blasphemy, Virgil, Dante's guide, says, "O Capaneus, by your insolence you are made to suffer as much fire inside as falls upon you. Only your own rage could be fit torment for your sullen pride."

John Ciardi, from whom this translation comes, notes that the root of blasphemy is inner violence, and this inner violence is what torments Capaneus more than the sands, which he interprets here as the wrath of nature, or the burning fires, a manifestation of the wrath of God. If this kind of sterility is the fate that awaits the blasphemers, what then of the atheists, like Farinata whom Dante meets in the sixth circle, who could not be bothered even to blasphemy? Dante demonstrates the literal holes they have dug for themselves by depicting them as lying forever in tombs that will be sealed on judgment day, for they professed the soul's mortality in life, and they receive what they sought in death. In both cases, God is good since he gives each person exactly what that person wills for himself.

The person of faith, though, prays that God's will be done, and that requires at the minimum true belief in a God to whom we can relate. True belief, though, flourishes only when we are zealous in sharing it with others. The reason is that those who do not prepare themselves to be able to talk of their faith and do not share their belief when there is opportunity are in part culpable for the unbelief of others that strengthens the secularization of society, a point *Gaudium et spes* explains:

> Undeniably, those who willfully shut out God from their hearts and try to dodge religious questions are not following the dictates of their consciences, and hence are not free of blame; yet believers themselves frequently bear some responsibility for this situation [. . . and . . .] can have more than a little to do with the birth of atheism. To the extent that they neglect their own training in the faith, or teach erroneous doctrine, or are deficient in their religious, moral or social life, they must be said to conceal rather than reveal the authentic face of God and religion. (§ 19)

It is no mystery, then, that a society steeped in the secular values of the Enlightenment would find itself fertile (sterile?) ground for the rise of the New Atheists, whose characteristics are both that it seeks to use scientific demonstration as its principal means of drawing conclusions on the existence of God and that it is highly political with an agenda to eradicate all theistic belief in the supernatural. What our possible futures might be under an atheist hegemony is the subject of narrative reasoning – whether the "dystopian" vision of George Orwell's *1984* where the power of the state crushes the soul of man or the "utopian" vision of Ayn Rand's *Anthem* where the soul of man overcomes the power of the state. We have only one future, though, under theism, and that is of infinite growth within an infinite being, the greatest blessing of our finitude, which can never plumb the depths of our Creator but only grow eternally in joyful communion with Him

The four horseman of the New Atheism may not be the best advocates for their position, but they are the most popular. The reason is that they are rather vague in comparison with the intellectual giant of an atheist Bertrand Russell. Their vagueness, though, has a purpose behind it, for too much specificity brings about greater scrutiny. One can exist in the gaps of a vague idea as every sympathetic reader will interpret it according to his or her own understanding and a greater chance of finding assent among them will occur. Edward Feser, author of *The Last Superstition: A Refutation of the New Atheism,* points out, like Robert Augros and George Stanciu, authors of *The New Story of Science,* that the real issue has never been the advances humans have made in the sciences; rather, the real issue has to do with two competing philosophical systems. What Augros and Stanciu call the Old Story, which concerns Enlightenment discoveries of nature's mechanics, is really a new story in the grand scheme of things. This story explores the mechanics of a purposeless material existence.

Feser identifies Rene Descartes as the first mechanic of the Enlightenment. It was out of Cartesian philosophical thinking, along with that of Hobbes, Locke, and Hume who followed him, after all, that this story arose. Descartes, though, did not intend to limit humankind to a purely material existence, nor did he intend to do away with God. He explains in the preface to his *Meditations*, a treatise written for the theological faculty at the Sorbonne, that his theory would strengthen religion against the claims of atheism. His splitting the mind and the body was meant to be a philosophical demonstration of the immateriality of the intellect, that even without sensory input the mind would still know that it exists because it is a thinking thing. The Islamic philosopher, Avicenna, had done a similar thought experiment many centuries prior to this in his explanation of the floating man, but Avicenna's ends were different. He was not trying to advance what would become under Descartes a theory of dualism of mind and body.

The old, old story was philosophical, not just scientific, and we find in the philosophical works of Plato, Aristotle, Augustine, and Aquinas a teleological perspective, a perspective that explains what philosophers call a final cause, an end toward which we are directed, a purpose for our being. It is out of this that we get a philosophy of nature, the first philosophical constructs that lead us into an understanding of the natural world, into a method in science. What Augros and Stanciu call the New Story of science, then, is really a return to that older story that philosophy had already demonstrated to us. Our science has demonstrated a big bang, for instance, and we find that the scientists also perceive an expanding universe to have had a beginning point. If that is the case, if both science and religion agree, taking into consideration Lemaître's point to Pope Pius XII, that at some time there was a beginning point, one has to wonder what brought it about. This is the philosophical question, "Why is there something, and not nothing?"

Questions like this cannot be answered by science because "why" questions are inherently philosophical whenever they ask about the formal or final causes. It's "how" questions that are understood as scientific, that look into the internal mechanics of a thing. They ask about the efficient and material causes. Guy Consolmagno, one of the chief astronomers at the Vatican Observatory, has written a book called *God's Mechanics: How Scientists and Engineers Make Sense of Religion*. In it, he explains how scientists, who are trained to be skeptics bent on figuring out how something works, can reconcile science with their faith.

After all, what the scientist is looking for is material evidence. The evidence for Christianity, though, is spiritual, and it lies in faith. As Hebrews 11:1 tells us, faith is "the substance of things hoped for, the evidence of things not seen." If faith is our evidence, then the disqualifiers upon which the empirical sciences are based do not apply since one cannot disprove that kind of evidence, like one can do in science, by pointing to its lack. All one can prove is that so and so does not have it. In short, faith that is lacking in one or more persons cannot cancel out faith that is present in one or more persons in the way that one science experiment can cancel out another science experiment.

After we figure out how something works, we always want to move to the next step and ask that "why" question. It is akin to the aha moment – the "okay, I've figured out how the entire universe operates . . . so, hmmm, why is it set up this way? What's its purpose?" The "why" question is inherently teleological. It resonates with the framework set up by the ancients. Any child of the Enlightenment who thinks that there is no purpose to the universe and, like Sartre, can see its existence only as an absurdity, cannot authentically ask the "why" question because it points to a teleological reality that they fundamentally cannot reconcile with their worldview.

It has been attributed to St. Augustine the idea that the book of nature and the book of revelation were written by the same author, and neither can be shown to be in conflict if both are properly understood. Both rely on our reason to understand, and because the defining characteristic of a human person is that he or she is a rational animal, we are already geared for this study. As rational beings with immaterial intellects, with immortal souls as the form of our bodies, we are called to engage our minds in the study of the natural world precisely because the order of knowledge leads us to an understanding of the order of being.

Perhaps it is for this reason that Aristotle begins his Metaphysics with the simple statement: "All men by nature desire to know." Someone like Richard Dawkins should not be averse to at least reading Aristotle since Aristotle did not know that the entity that he was describing was relational or that such an entity would have created out of love, except that Aristotle, though a pagan, understood metaphysical realities and the idea that something could exist outside of nature. That sort of an idea would be something that Dawkins would reject. In fact, were he to adopt it, it would undermine his position entirely. It is for this reason that Dawkins denies the simplicity of God and describes him in terms of irreducible complexity. A "simple" God, after all, can only be cast in terms of the supernatural, but by appealing to what must be his obvious complexity, Dawkins can gaze through his materialist worldview and cast God as a "natural" phenomenon, securing thereby a universe that can be explained wholly and entirely in material terms.

Philosophically rather than scientifically laid out, though, the order of knowledge aims for the universals. We come to understand through our senses, which we necessarily apply to the world around us. In so doing, we develop percepts that bring about concepts. For instance, we touch fire and perceive that it is hot, and from that perception, we develop the concept of hotness. We do not need to touch fire again to refresh our minds on what hotness is. Once is enough. That concept of hotness is a universal concept in that many particular things can inhere within it. This ability we have to grasp universals points to a transcendent capacity of the human intellect. We can move in this way along all three levels of philosophical abstraction – the first dealing with material things (or empirical science), the second dealing with quantifiable things (or mathematics), and the third dealing with non-material things (or metaphysics). Metaphysics, because it concerns non-material being, involves the study of being as being.

The study of being as being is an ontological one, but, as St. Thomas pointed out, for metaphysics to be an ontology, it has to also be a theology. The spirit of this assertion reappears in Saint John Paul II's encyclical *Fides et Ratio*, where he writes that "[f]aith and reason are like two wings on which the human spirit rises to the contemplation of truth; and God has placed in the human heart a desire to know the truth—in a word, to know himself—so that, by knowing and loving God, men and women may also come to the fullness of truth about themselves." The fullness of faith cannot be proclaimed without also proclaiming the fullness of reason. They are not only two wings with which we soar, but they are also the two legs on which we take our first steps toward flight. Many of us are hobbling along on one leg or the other, pursuing blind faith or faithless reason.

This brings us back to our definition as humans – that we are rational animals. This adjective "rational" says a great deal about us. It tells us foremost that we are thinkers. It also tells us that our thinking is for some purpose, that purpose necessarily being a pursuit of what is good. We often err, though, by choosing the good-for-my-appetites-right-now rather than the good-for-my-being-over-time-and-into-eternity. The fact is that we pursue the good because we want happiness. A proximate goal of life is material happiness. An ultimate goal is eternal happiness. Reason tells us that our intellects are immaterial, so they do not die with our bodies. Reason also tells us that our souls are immaterial and are the form of our bodies. Our souls, then, have eternal destinies, and our intellects, that by which we know of our existence and our identity, remain with the form that has its temporal existence in the physical bodies we are using at this very moment.

We do not need faith to know any of this, as Aristotle demonstrated it in all the knowledge he advanced without the light of Abrahamic revelation. What faith tells us, though, is far more important. It answers that teleological question. It answers where these souls go when our material bodies die in a way that is convincing to us. It offers the promise of the fulfillment of all desire in God.

Though all matter degenerates, the immaterial, the non-matter, remains in existence. Aristotle, a pagan who didn't know the Abrahamic God, yet knew that there was only one God, and he demonstrated this in a number of ways. One of these ways explains God as the unmoved Mover (for everything that moves has to be moved by something else but this cannot go on to infinite regression). In his *Physics*, Aristotle writes,

> Since there must always be motion without intermission, there must necessarily be something, one thing or it may be a plurality, that first imparts motion, and this first movement must be unmoved. (Book VIII, Ch. 6)

(Notice the "or it may be a plurality" that got out 350 years before the doctrine of the Trinity.)

Had Aristotle been exposed to revelation, he might have put two and two together on this one and said, "Wait a second – I know that the soul is immaterial and survives the death of the body, but I don't know where it goes, exactly. I know that the human person is a composite of material stuff and immaterial stuff, but I don't know how that composite retains its integrity unless it comes back together again at some point. I also know that there is one God who created all this, but I don't know that he knows me, personally. Now, all this revelation stuff just fell from somewhere. I wonder if there's something to this idea that we go back to that one God and that our souls reunite with our bodies. But for that to happen, this one God would have to be a person who created us out of love for our own sake."

That might have been enough to get Aristotle started. Revelation would have answered some other questions for him, like how our relationship with God was damaged through sin (Aristotle did not know about sin, the idea that we could personally offend our Creator, that we could turn away from our Creator toward the created thing) and how that sin was done away with (350 years after Aristotle died) by God's incarnation so that man could return to his state of joyful communion with God. Our faith, in this way, brings us to the fullness of truth. It closes the circle. It completes us. It is for this reason that we can affirm that the fullness of Truth is shown to us through the fullness of faith and the fullness of reason.

The same man who wrote *Fides et ratio* in 1998 was the primary author of another document published in 1965 as the Pastoral Constitution on the Church in the Modern World, entitled *Gaudium et spes*. He explains that

> [t]he root reason for human dignity lies in man's call to communion with God. From the very circumstance of his origin man is already invited to converse with God. For man would not exist were he not created by Gods love and constantly preserved by it; and he cannot live fully according to truth unless he freely acknowledges that love and devotes himself to His Creator. Still, many of our contemporaries have never recognized this intimate and vital link with God, or have explicitly rejected it. Thus atheism must be accounted among the most serious problems of this age, and is deserving of closer

examination. (§ 19)

If for no other reason than that they have provided us with thousands of pages of text, hundreds of hours of YouTube video footage, tens of thousands of pages of blogspace, and other ways of more closely examining the issue, we ought to be grateful to the New Atheists for enabling that closer examination of atheism for which the document calls. The purpose of that examination is easily understood, for "it is the function of the Church, led by the Holy Spirit Who renews and purifies her ceaselessly, to make God the Father and His Incarnate Son present and in a sense visible" (§ 21). The Church has, in fact, been given a great commission by the risen Christ, who said as recorded by Matthew,

> All authority in heaven and on earth has been given to me. Therefore go and make disciples of all nations, baptizing them in the name of the Father and of the Son and of the Holy Spirit, and teaching them to obey everything I have commanded you. And surely I am with you always, to the very end of the age. (Matt. 28:18-20)

We profess our faith, therefore, under this particular commandment as a way of our living the truth in love, for man, in addition to having been created for communion with God, is created for communion with man (Matt. 12:28-31). *Gaudium et spes* ends its instruction on this point by explaining that "such an ideal cannot be realized, however, apart from sincere and prudent dialogue" (§ 21) with believers and non-believers alike, and such dialogue requires active engagement on our part toward ameliorating the conditions in this world that would impede others and ourselves from fully realizing the relationship we can have with our Creator and with one another through the active presence of God in our lives.

Modern atheists have to be educated on this point, and we have a model for how to do this following the principles of inter-faith dialogue, which advances the inculturation idea of meeting the atheists on their home turf. A worldview in which this life is all there is brings about quite a different way of engaging in the world, after all, than a worldview in which we grow from this life into the fullness of our eternal destiny. It is unlikely that we will convince an atheist of Christian truth by arguing from within the Bible, but we can convince them by making arguments from their way of engaging in the world. The first step toward our doing this is for us to be conscious of equivocal speech. To do that, we have to cultivate an understanding not only the meaning of our own vocabulary but also the meaning of the same vocabulary in the mind of the person with whom we are speaking.

Our pursuing an understanding of that vocabulary, furthermore, helps us deal with the phenomenon of straw men. Straw men are easy to build. The hard part is for us to identify the straw men that others use as a foil in their arguments. Dawkins straw man God, for instance, is described in these terms in *The God Delusion:* "The God of the Old Testament is arguably the most unpleasant character in all fiction: jealous and proud of it; a petty, unjust, unforgiving control-freak; a vindictive, bloodthirsty ethnic cleanser; a misogynistic, homophobic, racist, infanticidal, genocidal, filicidal, pestilential, megalomaniacal, sadomasochistic, capriciously malevolent bully." What kind of straw man is this, we have to ask ourselves. If we can understand his nature, we can reverse engineer it back to the mental state of the individual who created it. Our finding out the nature of what the person is rebelling against enables us to develop a better understanding of the pain in that person's soul.

What is further needed in the case of a material reductionist like Richard Dawkins is to get him talking about his belief in a multiverse and point out that he is advancing an idea for which there is no method of empirical testing or to get him talking about memes and point out that such things have no material existence. Dawkins is more like Capaneus, though, than he is like Farinata. His is not a problem of the intellect but a problem of the will. He absolutely does not want, as Scott Hahn and Benjamin Wiker point out in their book *Answering the New Atheism*, there to be a God and is so prejudiced against the idea that not even a demonstration of his own incoherence might help him.

Why bother, then?

Because it might help others who would otherwise fall under Dawkins' sway. In his book *The God Delusion*, Dawkins is really shooting buckshot at his reader, peppering the reader with argument after argument, never stopping long enough to scratch the surface on any given one. He is not aiming for the serious intellectual like John Haught or Edward Feser, but is instead aiming for the undergraduate mind that has not yet been fully formed in its understanding of its own identity. Something needs to be done, after all, to protect all the college freshmen until they can grow in their understanding of the fullness of the truth to which faith and reason brings us.

Our active engagement might also lessen the degree of sarcasm we hear coming from the acolytes to the New Atheism. Dawkins himself cites Thomas Jefferson in defense of his own ridicule of faith, "Ridicule is the only weapon which can be used against unintelligible propositions. Ideas must be distinct before reason can act upon them; and no man ever had a distinct idea of the trinity. It is a mere Abracadabra of the mountebanks calling themselves the priests of Jesus." If ridicule is the only weapon, then reason is no longer being employed, just emotion wittily expressed. What these atheists are really doing, though, is demonstrating time and again a reaction against theism, and any group that does little more than react to a bigger phenomenon is doing little more than willingly placing its internal locus of control in the hands of an external group. In that sense, theism has already won out against them.

We should not, as Catholics, fear the persecution of the atheists as something that can destroy our Church. At one point in our history, we were persecuted by men of God, hypocrites though they had been labeled, and we were saved by a simple observation, almost scientific in its delivery, by Gamaliel to the Sanhedrin:

> Some time ago Theudas appeared, claiming to be somebody, and about four hundred men rallied to him. He was killed, all his followers were dispersed, and it all came to nothing. After him, Judas the Galilean appeared in the days of the census and led a band of people in revolt. He too was killed, and all his followers were scattered. Therefore, in the present case I advise you: Leave these men alone! Let them go! For if their purpose or activity is of human origin, it will fail. But if it is from God, you will not be able to stop these men; you will only find yourselves fighting against God. (Acts 5:36-9)

The Church, we have demonstrated these past two thousand years, is from God, but the New Atheism is not, and being of human origin, it will fail.

CPSIA information can be obtained at www.ICGtesting.com
Printed in the USA
BVOW08s0500110915

417217BV00002B/205/P